EASY ORIGAMI FOR KIDS

NAOKO ISHIBASHI

TUTTLE Publishing

Tokyo | Rutland, Vermont | Singapore

CONTENTS

Cute Animals

Insect Friends

Sweets Treats

Tempting Snacks

Planes, Trains, Trucks and Cars

Friendly Flowers

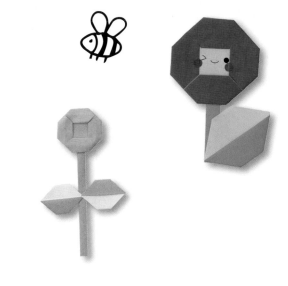

Before You Begin

Instructions

CUTE Animals

You can make your favorite animal origami here in the origami zoo! It's fun to fold up all the animals and pose them together. There's a cool lion, a cute penguin, an adorable panda and others. Which one will you fold first?

Typically ferocious, the king of beasts has become temporarily well mannered as it sits peacefully next to the tiger.

Tiger

Instructions on page 23

Lion

Instructions on page 25

This fox is taking a rest while an energetic squirrel cheers him up!

Fox

Instructions on page 26

Squirrel

Instructions on page 28

Kitten

Instructions on page 31

Cat

Instructions on page 31

Rabbit

Instructions on page 34

These cute animals are wonderful on their own, but their ribbons really set them apart.

Elephant

Instructions on page 35

These large and powerful animals don't typically coexist as pictured—let's hope they get along!

Bear

Instructions on page 37

Here are two popular animals sitting side by side! Their cocked heads enhance their cuteness.

Panda

Instructions on page 39

Koala

Instructions on page 41

Here come a couple of frosty favorites! The penguins are adorable—especially in a group.

Polar Bear

Instructions on page 43

Penguin

Instructions on page 44

These two are sprawled out lazily. The weather must be pleasant!

Dog

Instructions on page 45

Pig

Instructions on page 45

10

INSECT Friends

The insects have come to the world of origami to play as well! Not everyone likes to handle real insects, but they are very cute when they are made of paper.

Butterfly
Instructions on page ⭐47

Grasshopper
Instructions on page ⭐48

Dragonfly
Instructions on page ⭐49

Ladybug
Instructions on page ⭐48

Firefly
Instructions on page ⭐48

Caterpillar
Instructions on page ⭐50

Honeybee
Instructions on page ⭐51

SWEET Treats

With folded paper sweets and desserts, you can make as many as you want without fear of any tooth decay!

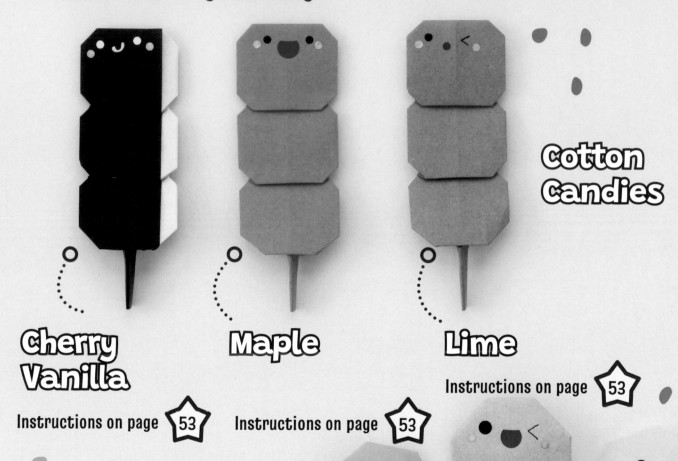

Cotton Candies

Cherry Vanilla

Instructions on page ⭐ 53

Maple

Instructions on page ⭐ 53

Lime

Instructions on page ⭐ 53

Here are cute cotton candies and lollipops. Give them each a different personality!

Lollipops

Instructions on page ⭐ 54

12

Plate

Instructions on page ⟨59⟩

Here is a tasty assortment of sweet snacks! Draw faces and arrange them any way you like!

Pudding

Instructions on page ⟨56⟩

Cupcake

Instructions on page ⟨55⟩

Donut

Instructions on page ⟨57⟩

13

TEMPTING Snacks

Make sure your origami diet is balanced! Fold up some of these pleasing paper portions.

> Here are some tasty seaweed and plum rice balls. It's fun to make snacks for your family!

Rice Balls and Plate

Instructions on page 58

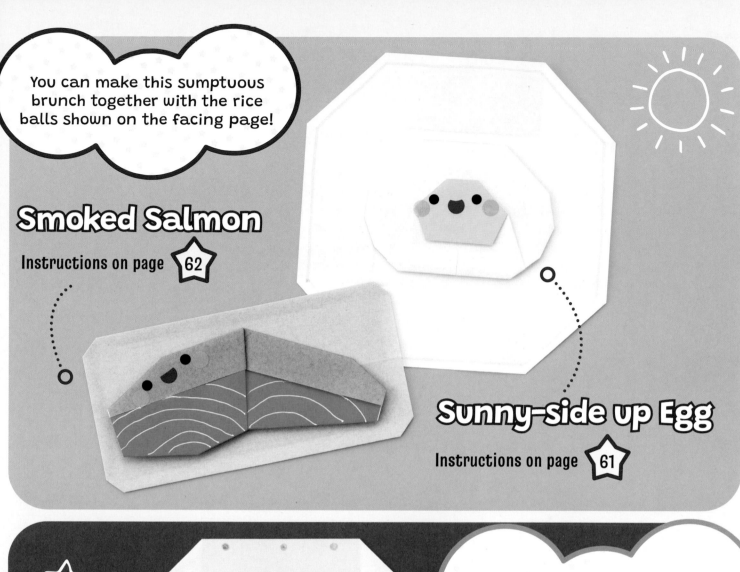

You can make this sumptuous brunch together with the rice balls shown on the facing page!

Smoked Salmon

Instructions on page 62

Sunny-Side up Egg

Instructions on page 61

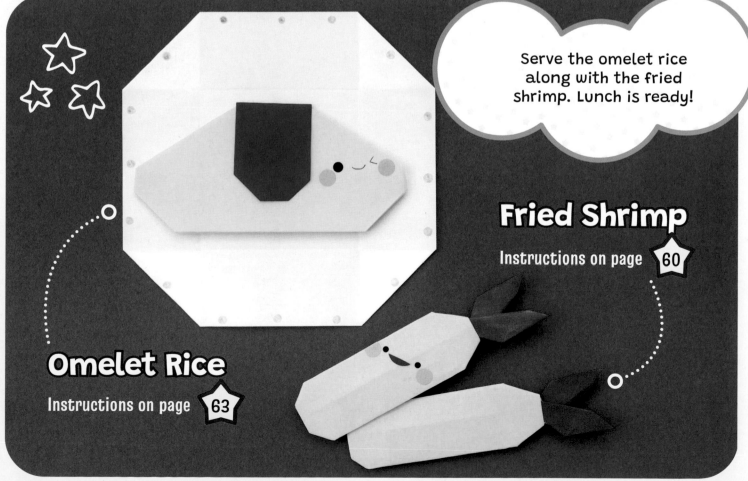

Serve the omelet rice along with the fried shrimp. Lunch is ready!

Fried Shrimp

Instructions on page 60

Omelet Rice

Instructions on page 63

Planes, Trains,

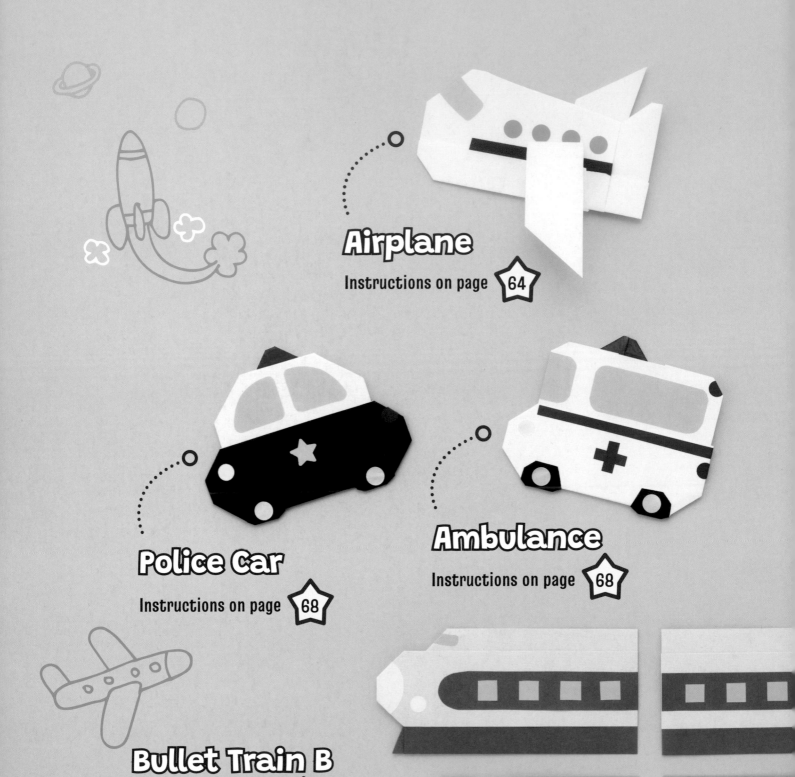

Airplane
Instructions on page ⭐64

Police Car
Instructions on page ⭐68

Ambulance
Instructions on page ⭐68

Bullet Train B
Instructions on page ⭐66

Trucks and Cars

Here are some common city vehicles. The bullet trains will get longer and longer as you add cars to the middle!

Backhoe

Instructions on page ⭐73

Fire Truck

Instructions on page ⭐71

Bullet Train A

Instructions on page ⭐66

17

FRIENDLY
Flowers

Make a colorful paper garden filled with many with different origami flowers. You can make bouqets with your favorite ribbons too!

Tulip

Instructions on page 76

Carnation

Instructions on page 75

Small Flower

Instructions on page 77

Poppy

Instructions on page 75

Before You Begin

This chapter will explain how to fold origami carefully, and it explains how to understand the symbols and techniques used in the model instructions, which start on page 23. Read this before you start folding the models.

Folding neatly

To make sharp-looking origami, pay attention to the following.

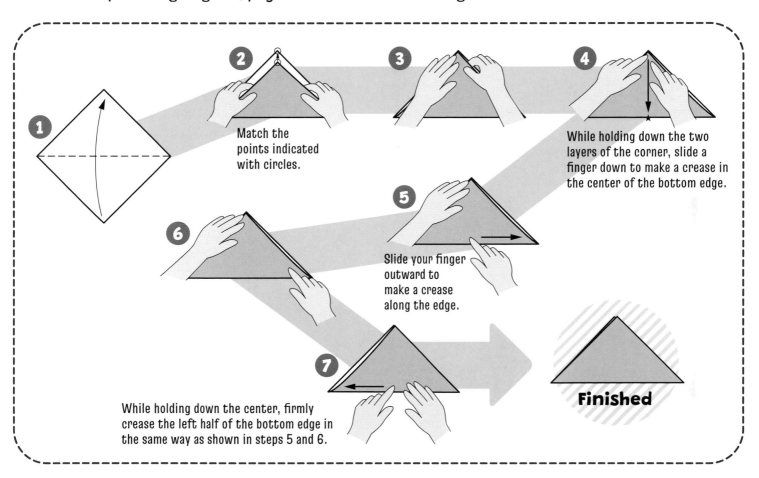

2 Match the points indicated with circles.

4 While holding down the two layers of the corner, slide a finger down to make a crease in the center of the bottom edge.

5 Slide your finger outward to make a crease along the edge.

7 While holding down the center, firmly crease the left half of the bottom edge in the same way as shown in steps 5 and 6.

Finished

Origami symbols and techniques

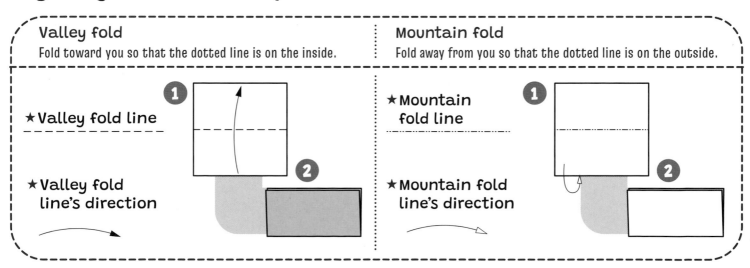

Valley fold
Fold toward you so that the dotted line is on the inside.

★ Valley fold line

★ Valley fold line's direction

Mountain fold
Fold away from you so that the dotted line is on the outside.

★ Mountain fold line

★ Mountain fold line's direction

Make a crease

Fold once and unfold.

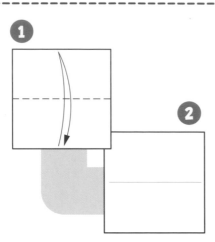

Spread the paper

Place your finger in the position of the white arrow. Then, open a pocket and squash the paper flat.

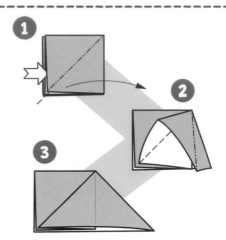

Turn over

Turn the paper over horizontally.

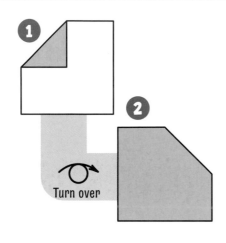

Rotate

Rotate the paper in a clockwise or counterclockwise direction.

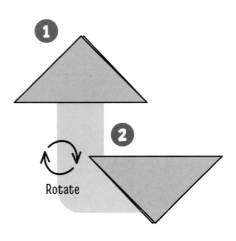

Zoom in

This symbol indicates that the following view is enlarged.

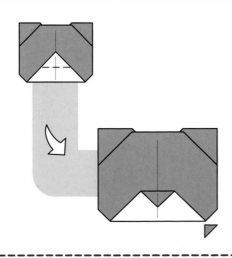

Step fold

Fold alternately with a valley fold and a mountain fold to pleat.

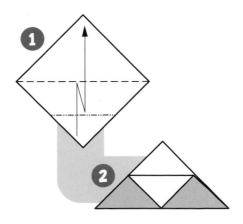

Inside reverse fold

Push a corner inside to invert it to the inside.

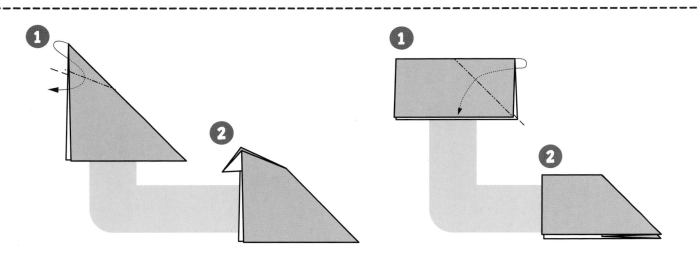

Insert tab into pocket

This symbol indicates that you should tuck a tab into a receiving pocket.

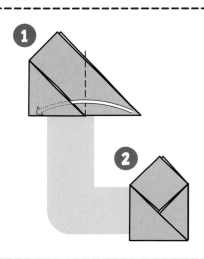

Outside reverse fold

Apply pressure to a corner to invert it to the outside. It is helpful to partially unfold the model to avoid tearing.

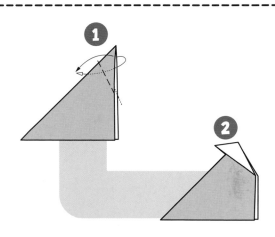

Equal divisions

This symbol indicates that the sections are of equal length.

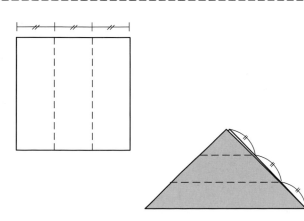

Hidden line/Virtual line

This shows a hidden line or the intended next flap position.

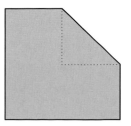

Basic Folding Methods

There are many origami models that rely on the same initial folds.
Shortcuts like this appear in this book, so here is a handy reference.

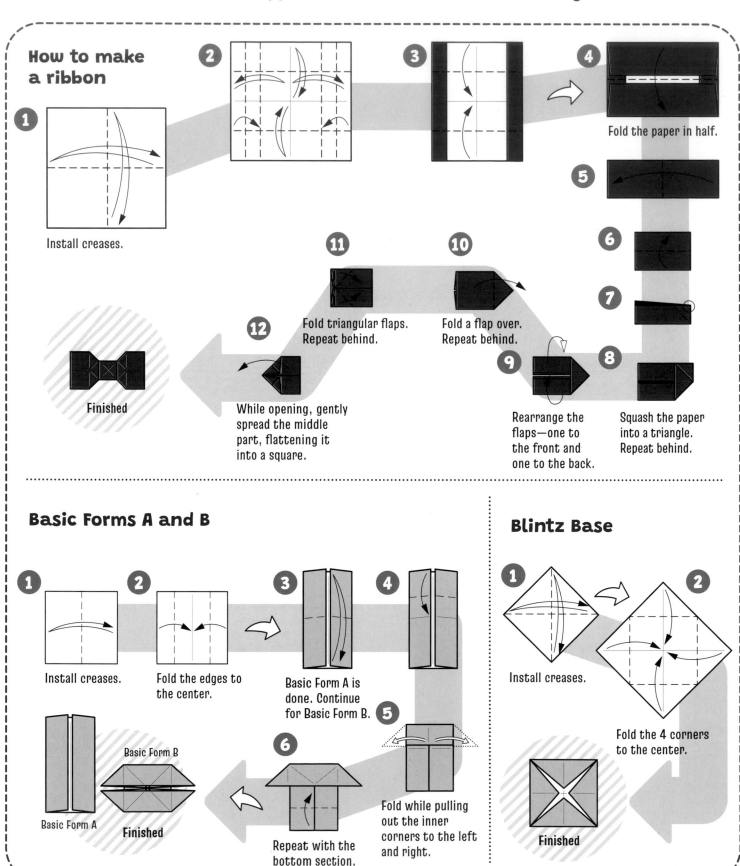

How to make a ribbon

1 Install creases.

2

3

4 Fold the paper in half.

5

6

7

8 Squash the paper into a triangle. Repeat behind.

9 Rearrange the flaps—one to the front and one to the back.

10 Fold a flap over. Repeat behind.

11 Fold triangular flaps. Repeat behind.

12 While opening, gently spread the middle part, flattening it into a square.

Finished

Basic Forms A and B

1 Install creases.

2 Fold the edges to the center.

3 Basic Form A is done. Continue for Basic Form B.

4

5 Fold while pulling out the inner corners to the left and right.

6 Repeat with the bottom section.

Basic Form A

Basic Form B

Finished

Blintz Base

1 Install creases.

2 Fold the 4 corners to the center.

Finished

22

Photo on page 4

Tiger

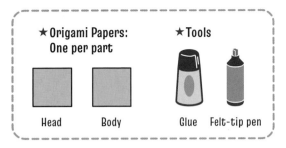

★Origami Papers:
One per part

Head   Body

★Tools

Glue   Felt-tip pen

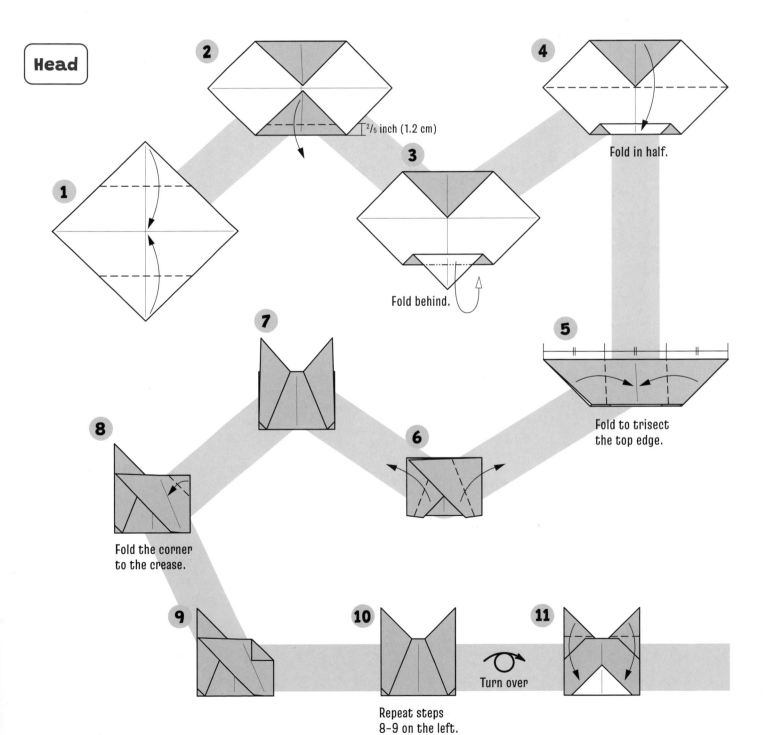

Head

1

2

²/₅ inch (1.2 cm)

3

Fold behind.

4

Fold in half.

5

Fold to trisect
the top edge.

6

7

8

Fold the corner
to the crease.

9

10

Repeat steps
8–9 on the left.

Turn over

11

13

12

Turn over

14

Turn over

15

The Head
is complete

Body — Refer to Basic Form A (page 22).

1
Fold outward.

2

3
Turn over

4
Fold behind. When folding, make the front side about 1/5 inch (5 mm) longer.

5
Split the upper part to the left and right.

6

7
Turn over

8
Fold the tip of the legs forward.

Fold the tip of the legs to point to the front.

The Body
is finished

How to assemble the parts

Draw the eyes.

Color in the nose.

Draw the pattern on the body.

✦ **The Tiger** ✦
is finished

Photo on page 4

Lion

★ Origami Papers:
One per part

Head	Mane	Body

★ Tools

Glue   Felt-tip pen

★ Tip
The Lion's head is folded the
same way as the Tiger's head
(page 23).

Mane

1
Fold the paper into a
triangle and make a
crease in the middle.

2
Fold the corners down
diagonally.
³/₄ inch (2 cm)   ³/₄ inch (2 cm)

3
³/₄ inch (2 cm)

The Mane
is finished

Body

1
Install creases.

2
Fold the top flap
behind.

3
Fold the paper into
a triangle.

4
Fold another triangle.

5
Squash the triangle
into a square.

6
Fold the bottom edge
to the back.

7
Fold the corners
behind.

The Body
is finished

How to assemble
the parts

Draw the eyes.

Color in the nose.

The Lion
is finished

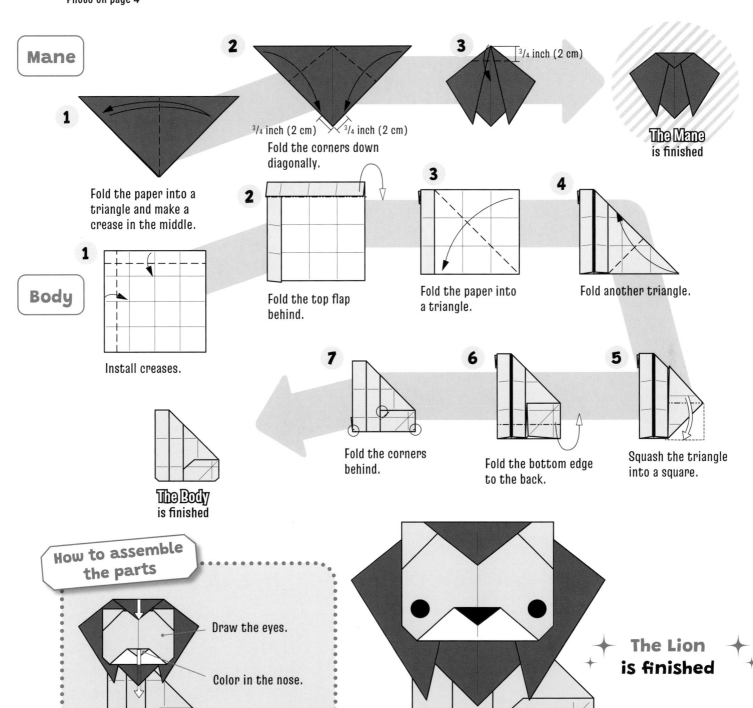

Fox

Photo on page 5

★ Origami Papers: One per part

Head   Body

★ Tools

Glue   Felt-tip pen

Head

1

³/₅ inch (1.5 cm)

Fold a triangle.

2

Fold the sides to the center.

3

Fold to the center and unfold.

4

Make a crease by folding the left and right edges inside to the center.

5

6

7

8

Fold the corners at the top of the head inside.

Turn over

The Head is finished

Body

1

Install creases.

2

3

Pull out the corners.

4

Turn over

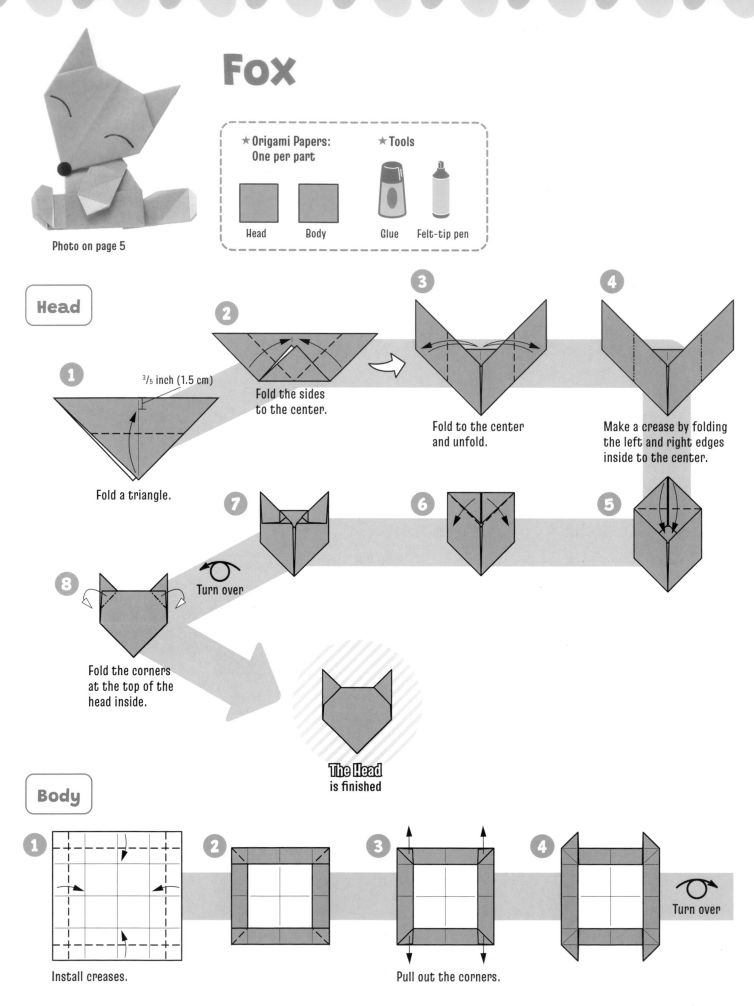

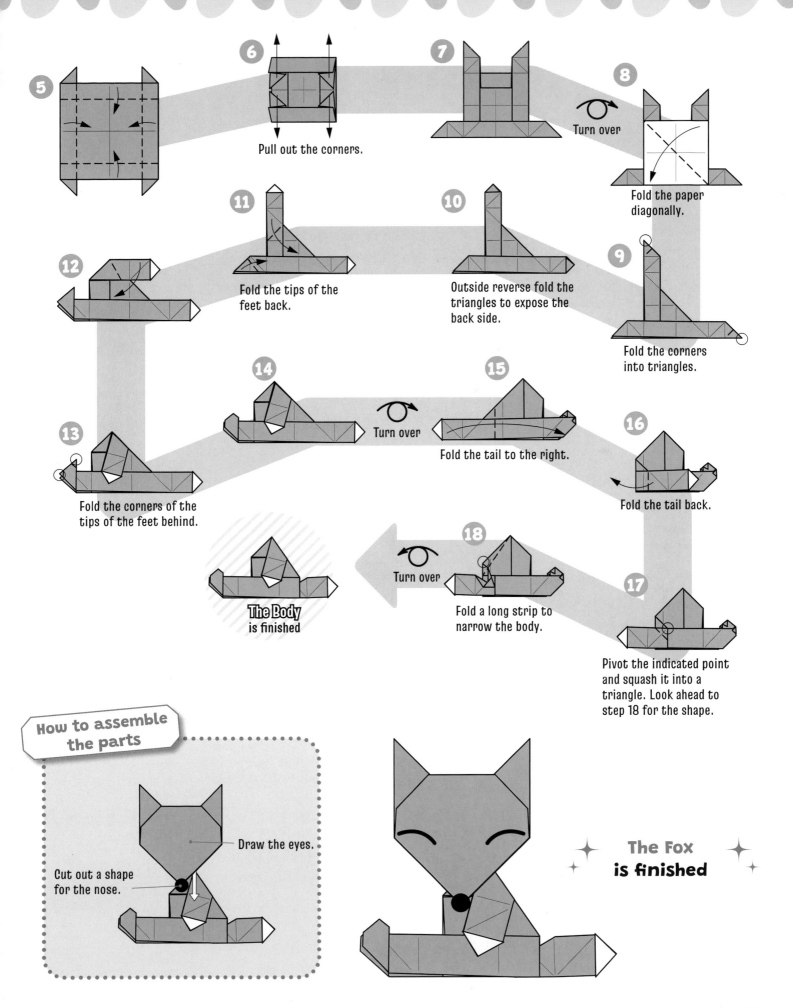

5

6
Pull out the corners.

7

8
Turn over
Fold the paper diagonally.

9
Fold the corners into triangles.

10
Outside reverse fold the triangles to expose the back side.

11
Fold the tips of the feet back.

12

13
Fold the corners of the tips of the feet behind.

14

15
Turn over
Fold the tail to the right.

16
Fold the tail back.

17
Pivot the indicated point and squash it into a triangle. Look ahead to step 18 for the shape.

18
Turn over
Fold a long strip to narrow the body.

The Body is finished

How to assemble the parts

Draw the eyes.

Cut out a shape for the nose.

✦ **The Fox** ✦
is finished ✦

Squirrel

Photo on page 5

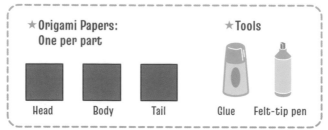

★ Origami Papers:
One per part

Head   Body   Tail

★ Tools

Glue   Felt-tip pen

Head

1 Make crossing creases on the paper, and then fold the lower part behind to the center.

2 Fold Basic Form A (page 22).

3

4 Open the inner part to form triangles, like an upside-down boat shape.

5

6 Fold the upper corner behind but leave about a $2/5$ inch (1 cm) portion of the flap showing.

$2/5$ inch (1 cm)

7 Fold the 2 sides up diagonally to form ears.

8 Fold back the corners.

Turn over

The Head is finished

Body

1 Fold the top edge behind.

2 Fold Basic Form A (see page 22).

3

4 Open the inner parts to form triangles, like boat shapes.

28

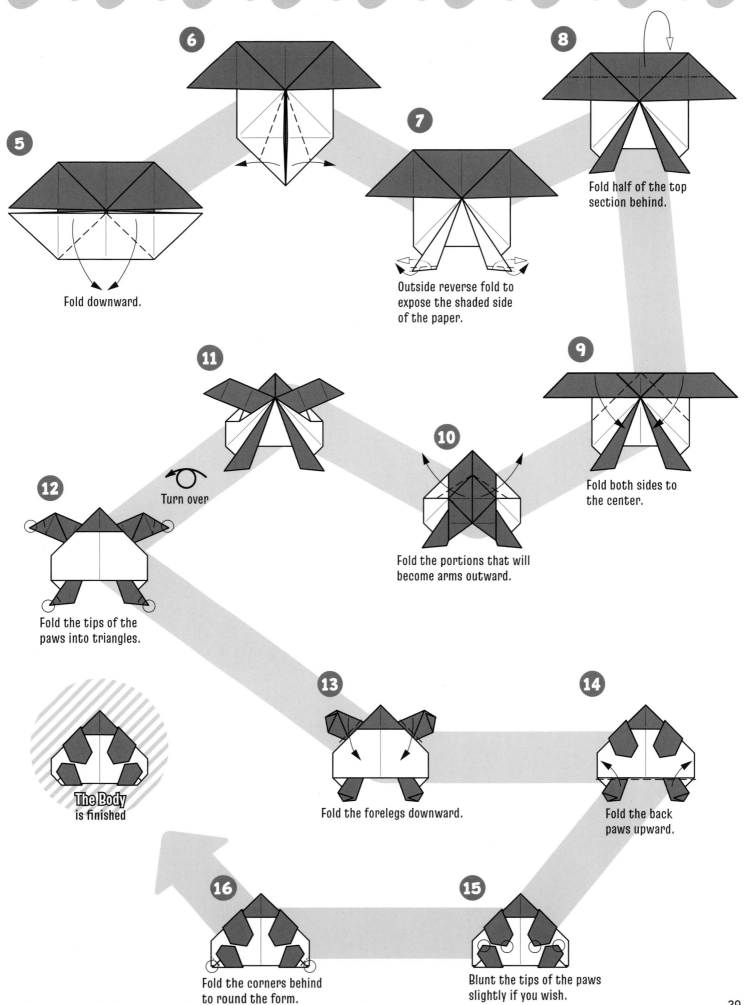

5 Fold downward.

6

7 Outside reverse fold to expose the shaded side of the paper.

8 Fold half of the top section behind.

9 Fold both sides to the center.

10 Fold the portions that will become arms outward.

11 Turn over

12 Fold the tips of the paws into triangles.

13 Fold the forelegs downward.

14 Fold the back paws upward.

15 Blunt the tips of the paws slightly if you wish.

16 Fold the corners behind to round the form.

The Body is finished

Tail

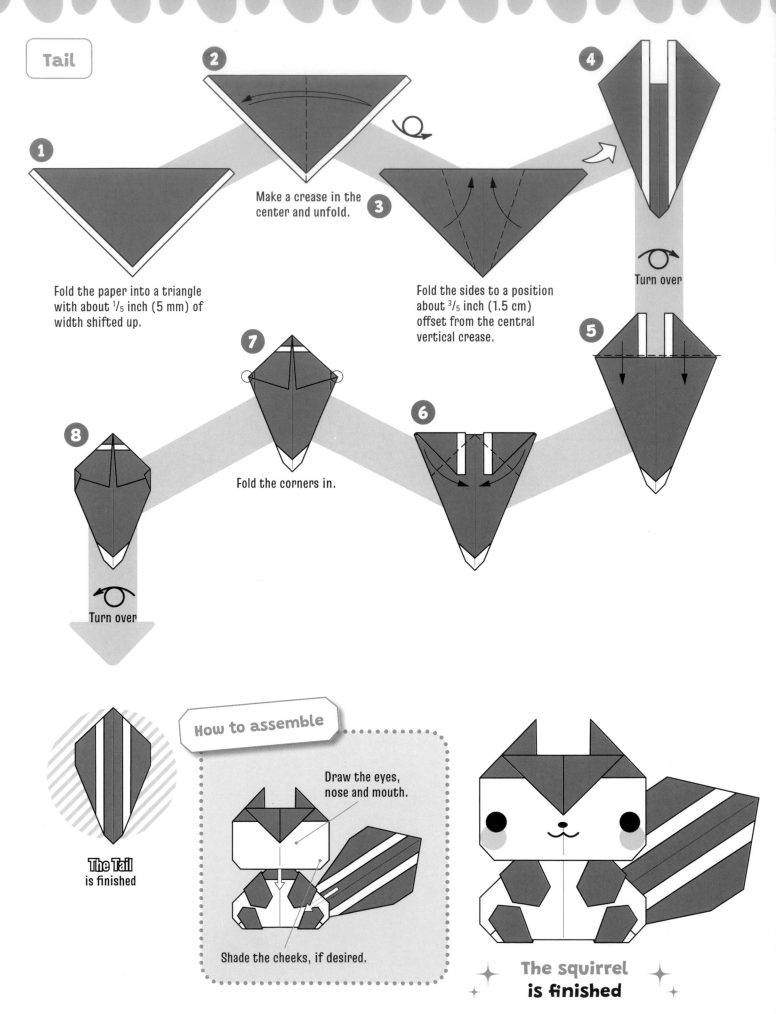

1
Fold the paper into a triangle with about 1/5 inch (5 mm) of width shifted up.

2
Make a crease in the center and unfold.

3
Fold the sides to a position about 3/5 inch (1.5 cm) offset from the central vertical crease.

4
Turn over

5

6

7
Fold the corners in.

8
Turn over

The Tail is finished

How to assemble

Draw the eyes, nose and mouth.

Shade the cheeks, if desired.

✦ **The squirrel** ✦ **is finished**

Photos on page 6

Kitten and Cat

★ **Origami Papers:**
One per part

| Head | Kitten body | Cat body | Ribbon |

★ **Tools**

Glue   Felt-tip pen

★ **Tips**
- The cats' heads are the same
- The ribbon-making instructions are on page 22. ★ ★

Head

1 Install creases.

2 Fold long, narrow triangles.

3 Turn over

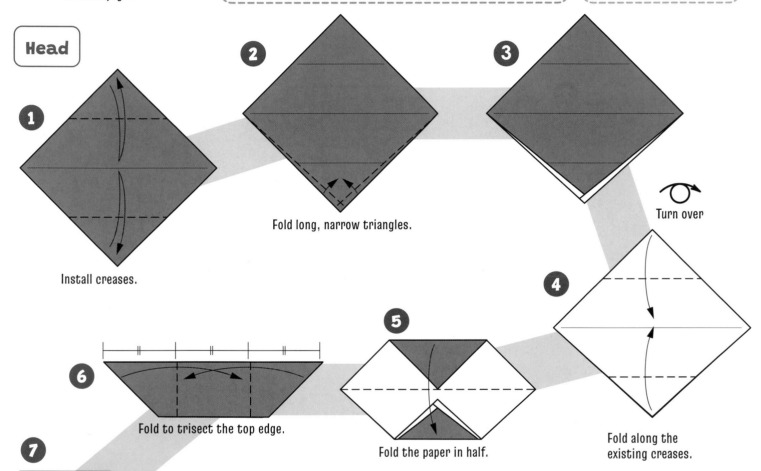

4 Fold along the existing creases.

5 Fold the paper in half.

6 Fold to trisect the top edge.

7

8 Fold the corners to round the cheeks.

9 Fold the corner to round the head. Repeat on the right. Turn over

The Head is finished

Kitten (Body)

Refer to Basic Form B (page 22).

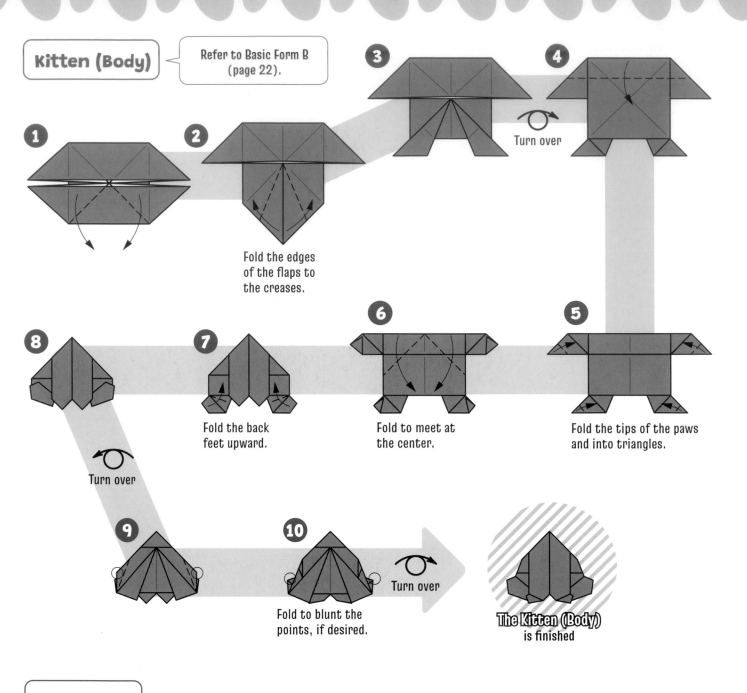

1

2 Fold the edges of the flaps to the creases.

3

4 Turn over

5 Fold the tips of the paws and into triangles.

6 Fold to meet at the center.

7 Fold the back feet upward.

8 Turn over

9

10 Fold to blunt the points, if desired.

Turn over

The Kitten (Body) is finished

Cat (Body)

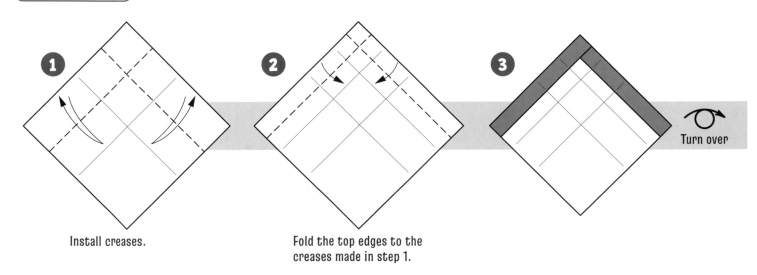

1 Install creases.

2 Fold the top edges to the creases made in step 1.

3 Turn over

④ Fold on the existing creases.

⑤

⑥ Turn over
Install a crease.

⑦ Fold the top edges to the center.

⑪ Turn over

⑩

⑨ Tuck the bottom triangular flap inside.

⑧

⑫

⑬ Turn over

⑭ Fold the tips of the feet.

Make the tips of the feet stand perpendicular to the body.

The Cat (Body) is finished

How to assemble

Color in the ears.

Draw the eyes.

Add the ribbon (refer to page 22).

Draw the pads on the back feet.

The Kitten/Cat is finished

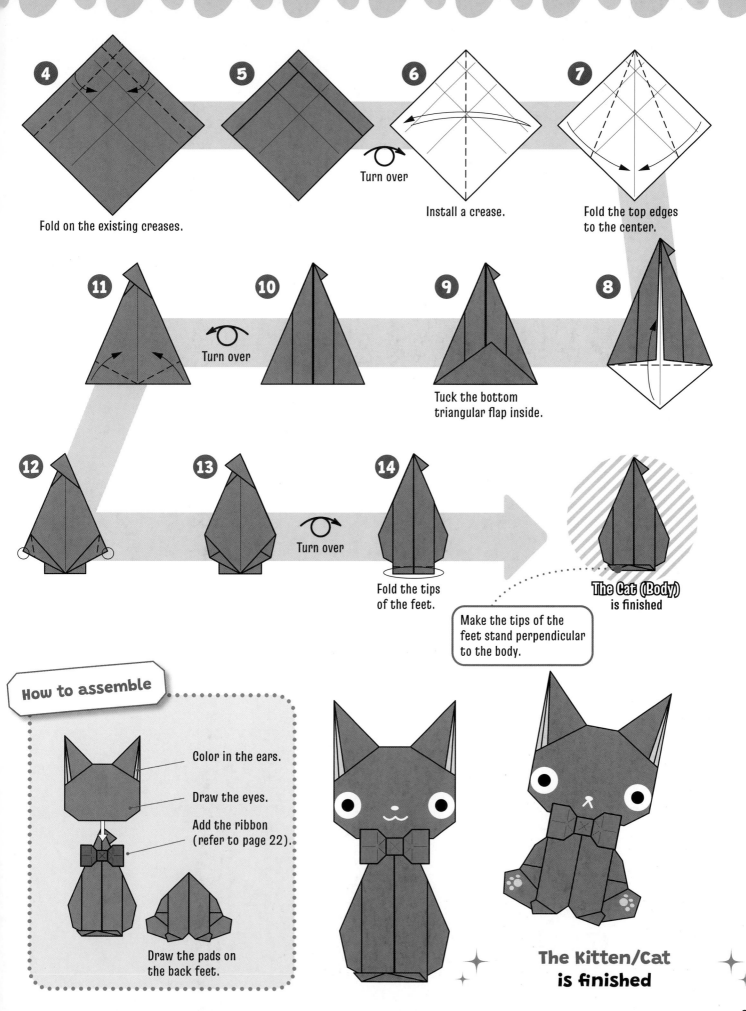

33

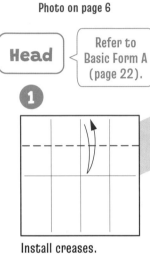

Rabbit

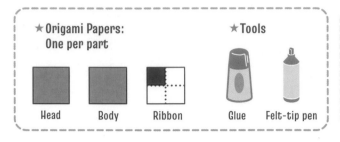

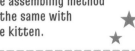

★Origami Papers:
One per part

Head	Body	Ribbon

★Tools

Glue   Felt-tip pen

★Tips
- The body is used as the same with the kitten on page 32.
- The assembling method is the same with the kitten.

Photo on page 6

Head Refer to Basic Form A (page 22).

1

Install creases.

2

Install more creases.

3

Turn over

4

5

Pull out the corners.

9

8

Pull the flaps to the outside.

7

Fold both sides toward the center.

6

Fold the top flap to the rear.

10

Fold the flaps upward diagonally.

11

Fold the bottom edge up to the crease from step 9.

15

Fold the tips of the ears a bit further

16

Turn over

14

Fold the tips of the ears into triangles

12

Tuck the flap inside.

13

Fold the corners to round the head.

The Head is finished

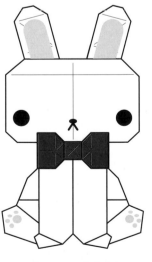

✦ **The Rabbit is finished** ✦

Elephant

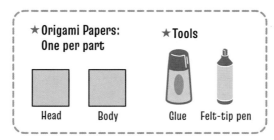

Photo on page 7

★ Origami Papers:
One per part

Head Body

★ Tools

Glue Felt-tip pen

Head

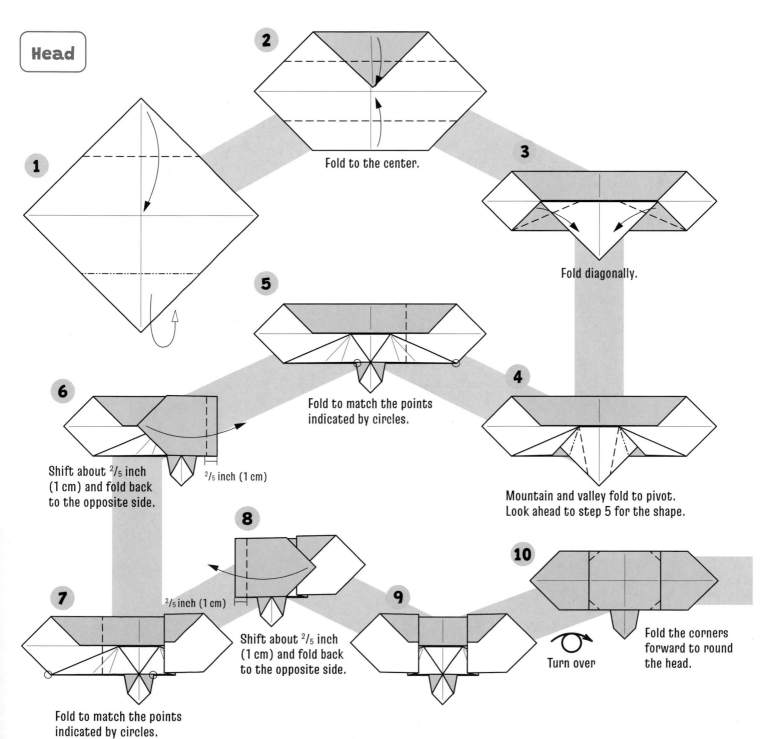

1

2
Fold to the center.

3
Fold diagonally.

4
Mountain and valley fold to pivot.
Look ahead to step 5 for the shape.

5
Fold to match the points
indicated by circles.

6
Shift about ²/₅ inch
(1 cm) and fold back
to the opposite side.

²/₅ inch (1 cm)

7
Fold to match the points
indicated by circles.

8
Shift about ²/₅ inch
(1 cm) and fold back
to the opposite side.

²/₅ inch (1 cm)

9
Turn over

10
Fold the corners
forward to round
the head.

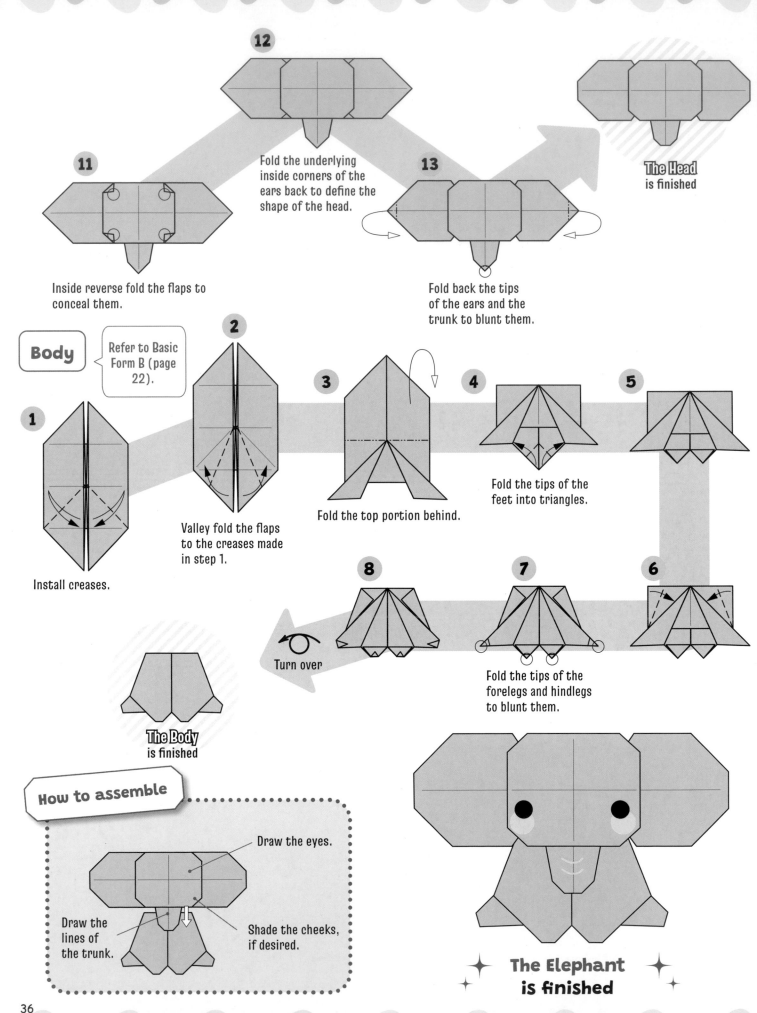

12

Fold the underlying inside corners of the ears back to define the shape of the head.

11

Inside reverse fold the flaps to conceal them.

13

Fold back the tips of the ears and the trunk to blunt them.

The Head is finished

Body | Refer to Basic Form B (page 22).

1

Install creases.

2

Valley fold the flaps to the creases made in step 1.

3

Fold the top portion behind.

4

Fold the tips of the feet into triangles.

5

6

7

Fold the tips of the forelegs and hindlegs to blunt them.

8

Turn over

The Body is finished

How to assemble

Draw the eyes.

Draw the lines of the trunk.

Shade the cheeks, if desired.

✦ **The Elephant is finished** ✦

Photo on page 7

Bear

★ Origami Papers:
One per part

Head	Body

★ Tools

Glue   Felt-tip pen

Head

1
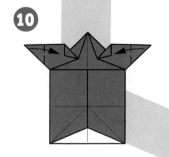

Install creases.

2

Fold the bottom corners
to meet the creases
made in step 1.

3
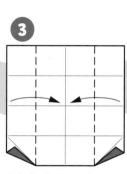

Fold Basic Form A
(refer to page 22).

4
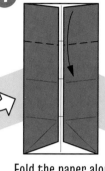

Fold the paper along
the existing crease.

5
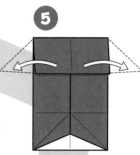

Pull out the inner
parts and fold them
into triangles. The
flap will resemble an
upside-down boat.

6
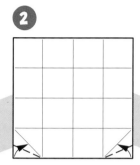

7
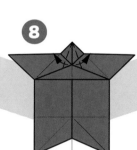

Fold to bisect
the angles.

8

9
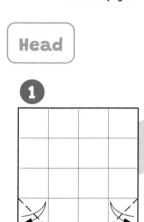

Pull to re-form
the shape of the
head. Look ahead
to step 10.

10
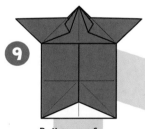

11
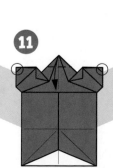

Fold the corners of the head
and ears to blunt them.

12
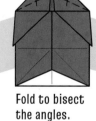

13
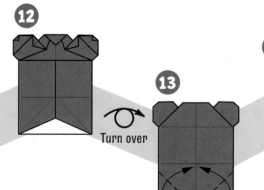

Turn over

³/₅ inch (1.5 cm)

Fold both bottom corners upward leaving
³/₅ inch (1.5 cm) of space in the center.

14
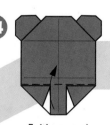

Fold upward.

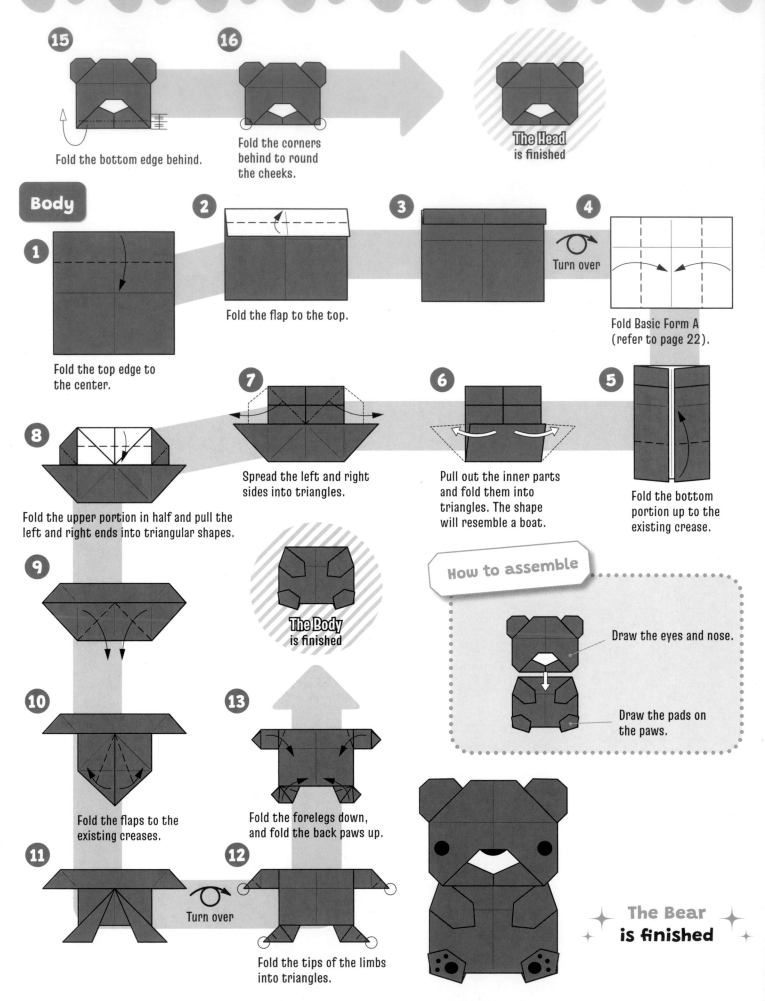

15 Fold the bottom edge behind.

16 Fold the corners behind to round the cheeks.

The Head is finished

Body

1 Fold the top edge to the center.

2 Fold the flap to the top.

3

4 Fold Basic Form A (refer to page 22).

Turn over

5 Fold the bottom portion up to the existing crease.

6 Pull out the inner parts and fold them into triangles. The shape will resemble a boat.

7 Spread the left and right sides into triangles.

8 Fold the upper portion in half and pull the left and right ends into triangular shapes.

9

10 Fold the flaps to the existing creases.

11

Turn over

12 Fold the tips of the limbs into triangles.

13 Fold the forelegs down, and fold the back paws up.

The Body is finished

How to assemble

Draw the eyes and nose.

Draw the pads on the paws.

The Bear is finished

Panda

Photo on page 8

★ Origami Papers:
One per part

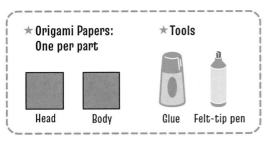

Head Body

★ Tools

Glue Felt-tip pen

Head ─ Refer to Basic Form A (page 22).

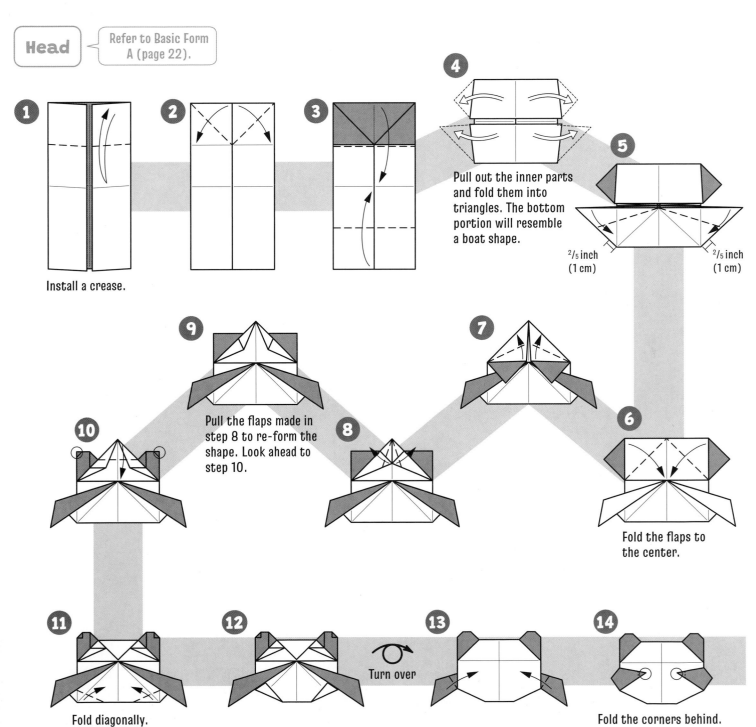

1 Install a crease.

2

3

4 Pull out the inner parts and fold them into triangles. The bottom portion will resemble a boat shape.

5 ²/₅ inch (1 cm) ²/₅ inch (1 cm)

6 Fold the flaps to the center.

7

8

9 Pull the flaps made in step 8 to re-form the shape. Look ahead to step 10.

10

11 Fold diagonally.

12

13 Turn over

14 Fold the corners behind.

15

16

Tug the bottom of
the ears to angle
them outward a bit.

The Head
is finished

Body

1 Install creases.

2 Fold the corners
into triangles.

3 Pull out the
corners.

4

Turn over

5

6 Pull out the corners.

7 Fold upward.

8 Fold the flaps that will
become the tips of the
back feet into triangles.

9

Turn over

10 Fold the tips of the
forelimbs into triangles.

11 Fold down to form shoulders.

12 Fold the tips of the paws in a
bit to blunt them.

How to assemble

Draw the eyes

The body
is finished

The Panda
is finished

40

Photo on page 8

Koala

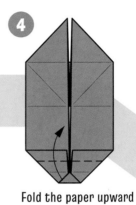

★ **Origami Papers:** One per part

Head	Body

★ **Tools**

Glue   Felt-tip pen

Head ‹ Refer to Basic Form B (page 22).

1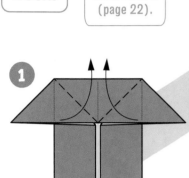

2

3

4

5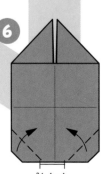

Fold the paper upward at the one-quarter mark indicated in step 3.

Turn over

6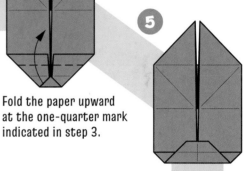

³/₄ inch (2 cm)

7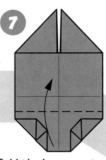

Fold the lower part up toward the center—this will determine the position of the nose.

8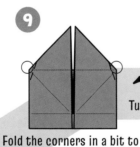

Turn over

9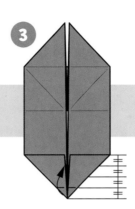

Fold the corners in a bit to slope the sides of the face.

10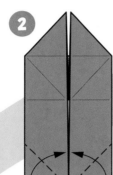

²/₅ inch (1 cm)

11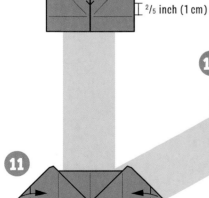

12

Fold the corners in to round the jaw.

13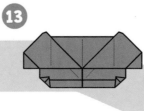

Turn over

The Head is finished

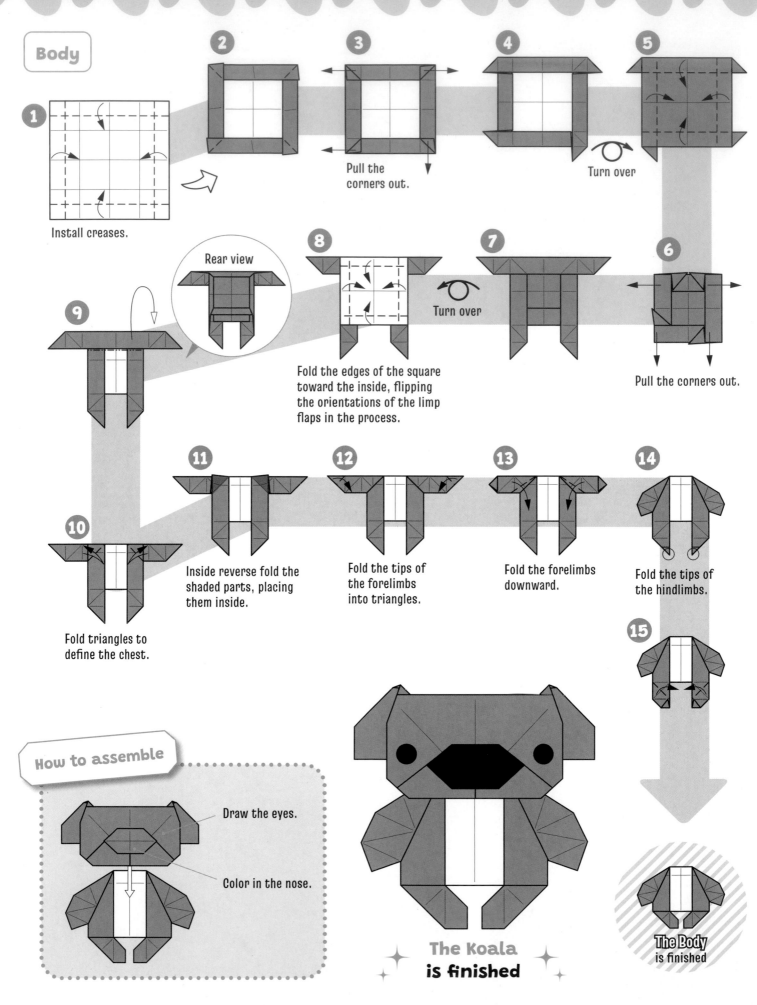

Body

① Install creases.

②

③ Pull the corners out.

④ Turn over

⑤

⑥ Pull the corners out.

⑦

⑧ Fold the edges of the square toward the inside, flipping the orientations of the limp flaps in the process.

Turn over

Rear view

⑨

⑩ Fold triangles to define the chest.

⑪ Inside reverse fold the shaded parts, placing them inside.

⑫ Fold the tips of the forelimbs into triangles.

⑬ Fold the forelimbs downward.

⑭ Fold the tips of the hindlimbs.

⑮

How to assemble

Draw the eyes.

Color in the nose.

The Koala is finished

The Body is finished

Photo on page 9

Polar Bear

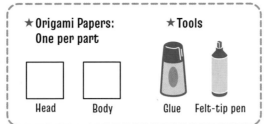

★ Origami Papers:
One per part

Head	Body

★ Tools

Glue   Felt-tip pen

★ Tip

Refer to the head-folding instructions for the Bear on page 37.

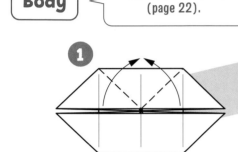

Body   Refer to Basic Form B (page 22).

1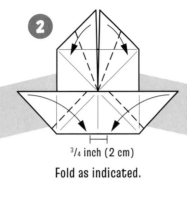

2

³/₄ inch (2 cm)

Fold as indicated.

3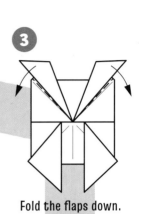

Fold the flaps down.

4

Fold in the corners.

5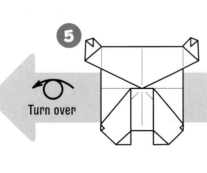

Turn over

The Body is finished

How to assemble

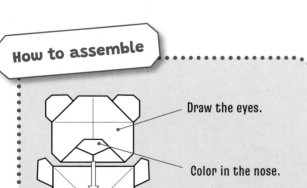

Draw the eyes.

Color in the nose.

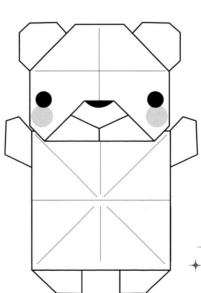

★ **The Polar Bear** ★
is finished

Penguin

Photo on page 9

★ Origami Papers:
One per part

Head   Body

★ Tools

Glue   Felt-tip pen

★ Tips

• Use the body folding method for the Koala up to step 14 (page 42).
• The assembly method is the same as the Koala's. ★

Head

Refer to Basic Form A (page 22).

1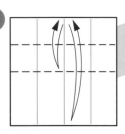
Install creases.

2
Fold diagonally to pair the points indicated with circles.

3

4

5
Fold Basic Form A.
Turn over

6

7
Fold upward along the existing crease.

8
3/5 inch (1.5 cm)

9

10
Turn over

11
Fold the corners behind, and then fold the beak part downward.

The Head is finished

Body

See the Koala body instructions on page 42.

1
Open the leg up a little so that the foot paper doesn't tear.
Fold the legs into triangles.

2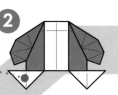
Gently turn the paper for the feet inside out, showing the back of the paper.

3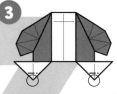
Fold the corners of the feet behind.

The Body is finished

Color the feet yellow.

Draw a bow tie for a cute effect!

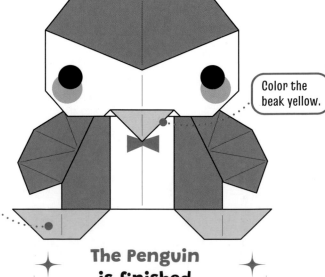

Color the beak yellow.

The Penguin is finished

Dog and Pig

★ **Origami Papers:** One per part

Head   Body

★ **Tools**

Glue   Felt-tip pen

★ **Tip**
The body parts of the two models are folded the same way.

Photos on page 10

Dog (Head)

1
³/₅ inch (1.5 cm)

Fold both layers upward, leaving about ³/₅ inch (1.5 cm) distance from the corner to the top edge.

2
Move the top triangular flap to the inside.

3
Fold half of the flap underneath.

4

Turn over

5
³/₄ inch (2 cm)

6
Fold the flaps to the center.

7
Re-fold the flaps from step 1 to the inside.

8

9
Turn over

10
Fold the ears downward.

11
Fold the ear tips and bottom of the jaw behind.

The Dog (Head) is finished

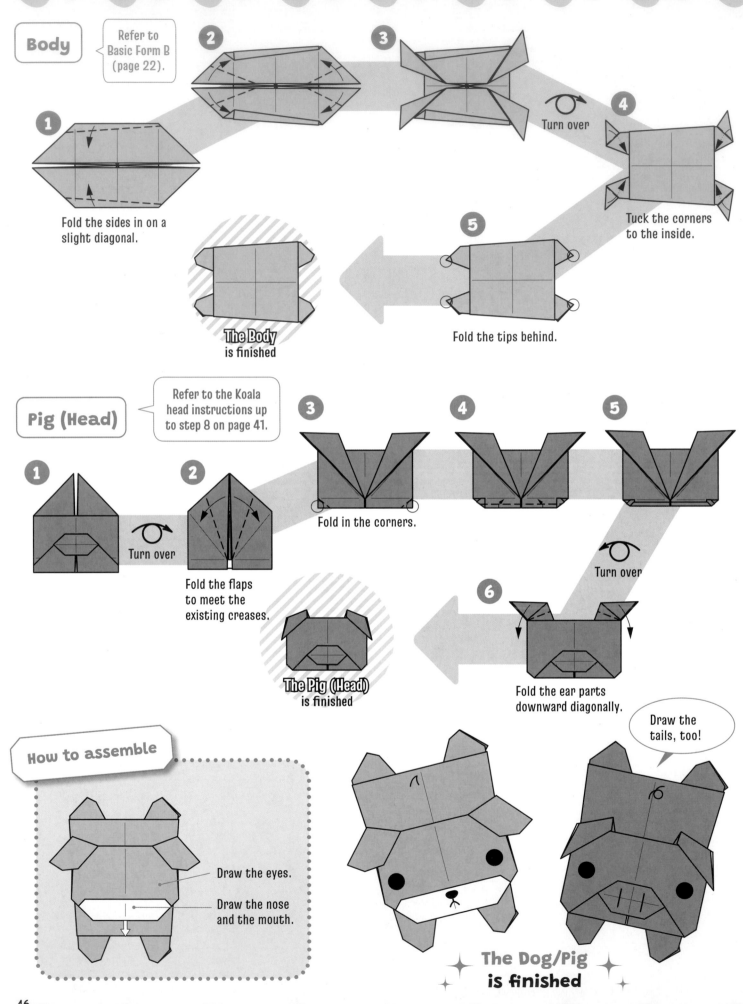

Body — Refer to Basic Form B (page 22).

1 Fold the sides in on a slight diagonal.

2

3 Turn over

4 Tuck the corners to the inside.

5 Fold the tips behind.

The Body is finished

Pig (Head) — Refer to the Koala head instructions up to step 8 on page 41.

1

2 Turn over — Fold the flaps to meet the existing creases.

3 Fold in the corners.

4

5

Turn over

6 Fold the ear parts downward diagonally.

The Pig (Head) is finished

How to assemble

Draw the eyes.

Draw the nose and the mouth.

Draw the tails, too!

The Dog/Pig is finished

Butterfly

Photo on page 11

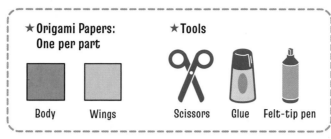

★Origami Papers: One per part

Body Wings

★Tools

Scissors Glue Felt-tip pen

Body

Refer to the Basic Form A (page 22).

1 Make a crease at the halfway point, and then fold the top edge down so the crease is made at one-third of the distance to the middle horizontal crease.

2 Fold behind.

3 ³/₄ inch (2 cm)

4 Step fold.

Turn over

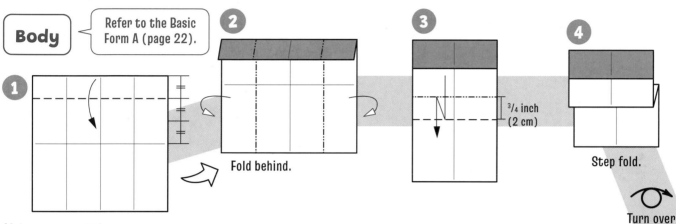

5 Fold the sides to the center, and then squash the parts that will not lie flat into triangles.

6 Turn over

7 Fold the corners behind.

The Body is finished

Wings

1 Fold in half, and then in half again.

2 Open the square and squash it into a triangle.

3

4 Turn over — Open the square and squash it into a triangle.

5 Fold in half.

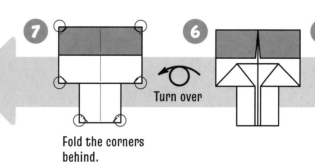

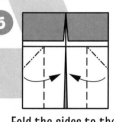

6 Fold the top layers downward diagonally.

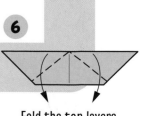

7 Fold the lower corners just a bit

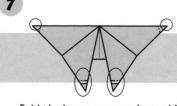

The wings are finished

Assembling methods are on page 52

Photos on page 11

Grasshopper, Ladybug and Firefly

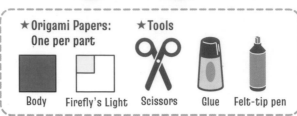

★Origami Papers:
One per part

Body | Firefly's Light

★Tools

Scissors | Glue | Felt-tip pen

★Tip

The Grasshopper, Ladybug and Firefly body units are the same.

Body — Refer to Basic Form A (page 22).

1

Install creases and fold the upper edge down.

2
Fold to pair the points indicated by circles.

3
Fold behind.

4
Step fold.

5
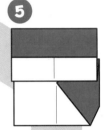

Turn over

6
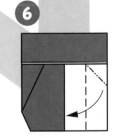
Fold the right side to the center, and then squash the part that will not lie flat into a triangle.

7
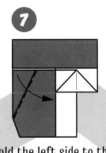
Fold the left side to the center, and then squash the part that will not lie flat into a triangle.

8
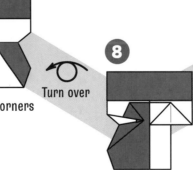
Turn over

9
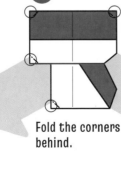
Fold the corners behind.

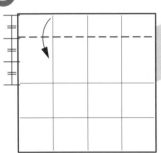

The Body is finished

Firefly's light

1
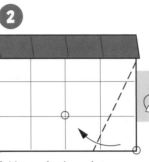
Fold the four corners to the center (Blintz Base).

2
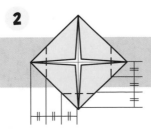

3

Turn over

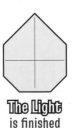
The Light is finished

Dragonfly

★ Origami Papers: One per part
★ Tools

Body Wings   Scissors Glue Felt-tip pen

Photo on page 11

Body

Refer to Basic Form A (page 22).

1 Install creases and fold the upper edge down.

2 Fold both sides to the center.

3 Step fold.

4 Fold to the center, and then squash the parts that will not lie flat into triangles.

5

6 Fold the corners behind.

Turn over

The Body is finished

Wings

Refer to Basic Form B (page 22).

1

2 Fold to the center.

Turn over

3

4

Turn over

The Wings are finished

The assembly instructions are on page 52.

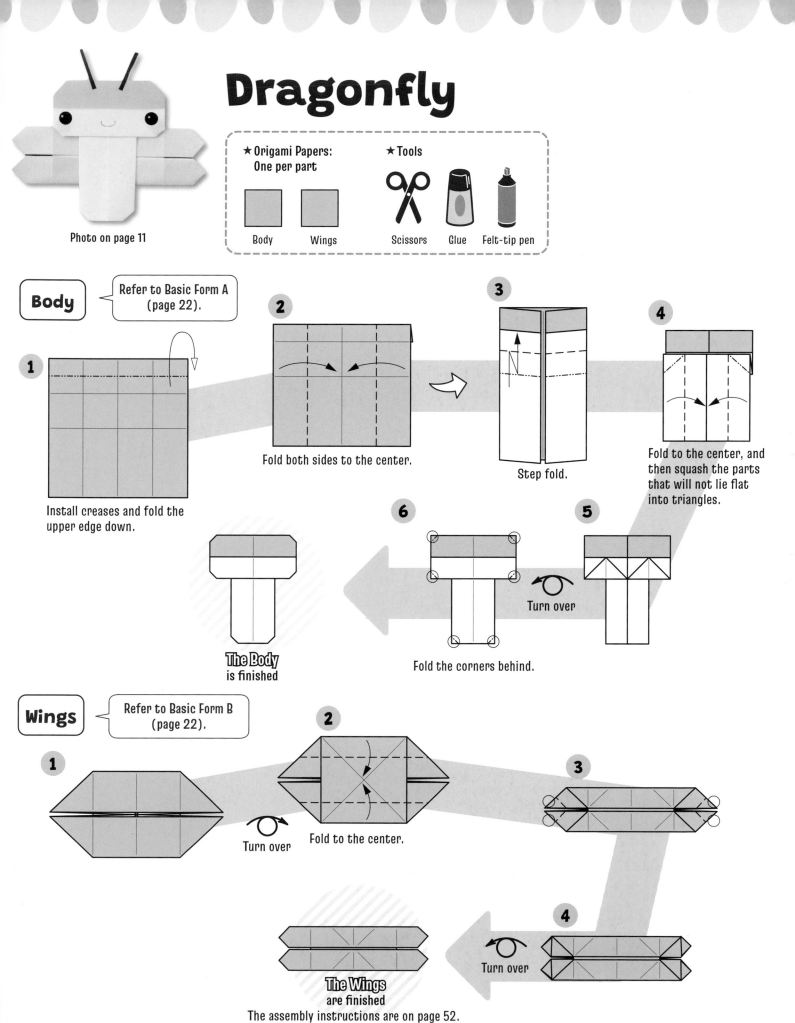

Photo on page 11

Caterpillar

★Origami Papers:
  One per Caterpillar

★Tool

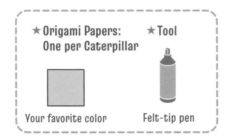

Your favorite color

Felt-tip pen

Refer to Basic Form A
(page 22).

1

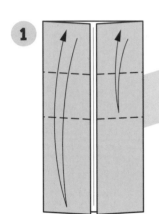

Install creases.

2

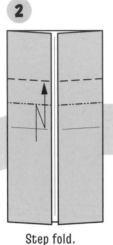

Step fold.

3

Fold the sides in to the
center, and then squash
the parts that will not
lie flat into triangles.

4

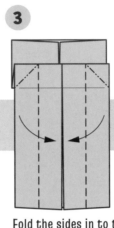

5

6

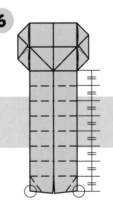

Crease into 8 sections
and narrow the end of
the body.

7

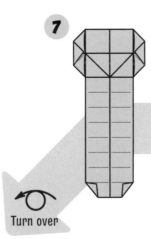

Turn over

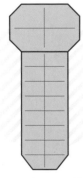

**The Caterpillar
is finished**

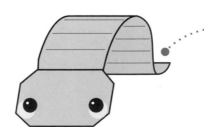

Curl the Caterpillar into
an arched shape. Now it's
ready to pose and play!

50

Honeybee

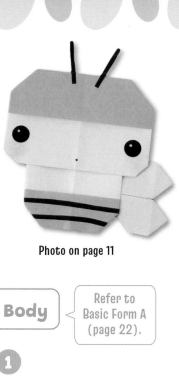

Photo on page 11

★ Origami Papers:
One per part

Body	Wings

★ Tools

Scissors Glue Felt-tip pen

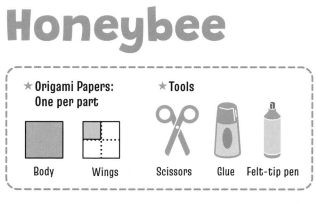

Body — Refer to Basic Form A (page 22).

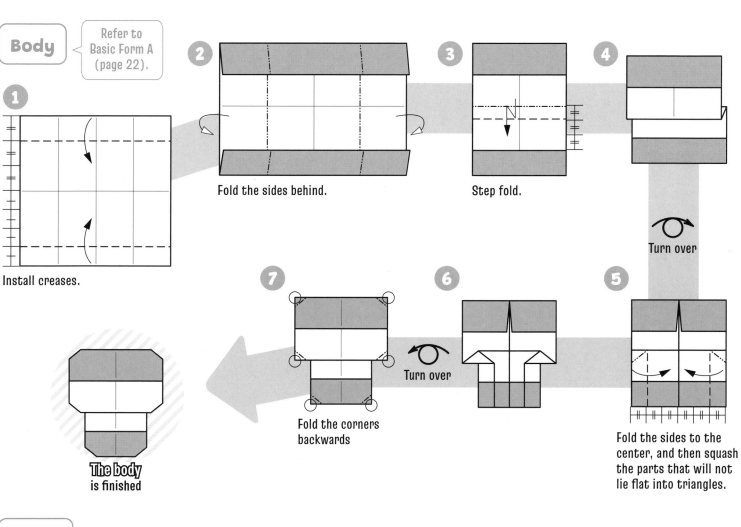

1 Install creases.

2 Fold the sides behind.

3 Step fold.

4

Turn over

5 Fold the sides to the center, and then squash the parts that will not lie flat into triangles.

6 Turn over

7 Fold the corners backwards

The body is finished

Wings

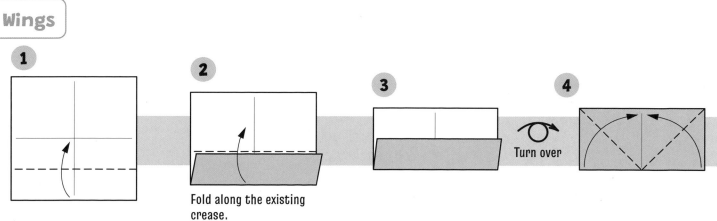

1

2 Fold along the existing crease.

3

4 Turn over

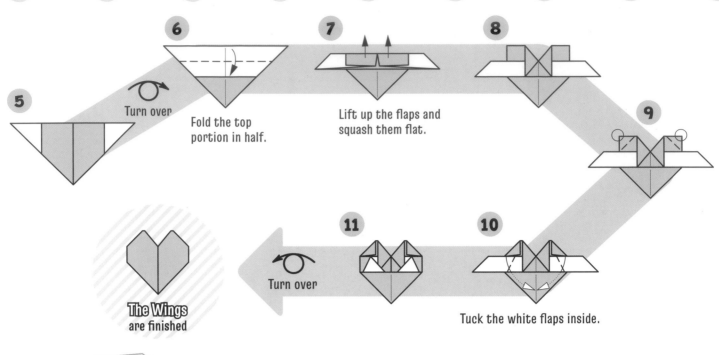

5

6 Fold the top portion in half.

Turn over

7 Lift up the flaps and squash them flat.

8

9

10 Tuck the white flaps inside.

11

Turn over

The Wings are finished

How to assemble

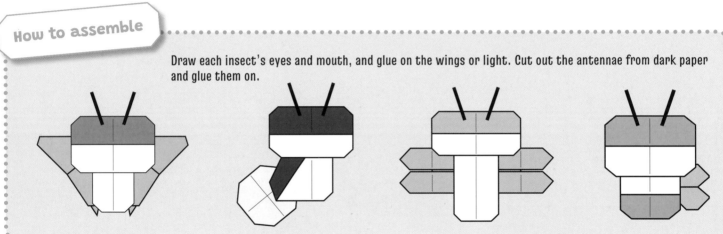

Draw each insect's eyes and mouth, and glue on the wings or light. Cut out the antennae from dark paper and glue them on.

✦ **The Insect** ✦
✦ **Origami Models** ✦
are finished

Photos on page 12

Cotton Candies

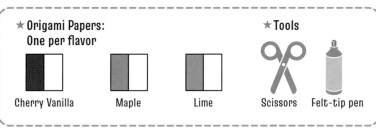

★ Origami Papers:
One per flavor

Cherry Vanilla   Maple   Lime

★ Tools

Scissors   Felt-tip pen

Cherry Vanilla

1 **2** **3**

The Cherry Vanilla paper is ready (turn it over and proceed to step 2, below).

Maple/Lime

1

2 Make mountain folds.

3 Make step folds.
¹/₅ inch (5 mm)

4 Raise the bottom flap.

5 Increase the pleat to ²/₅ inch (1 cm) in length and fold it back down.

6

7 Turn over
Fold in the corners.

8 Reverse the folds from step 7 to tuck the corners inside.

9

10 Turn over
Fold in the corners.

11

12 Turn over
Roll to narrow the paper cone part to taste.

Draw faces for a cute finishing touch.

The Cotton Candies are finished

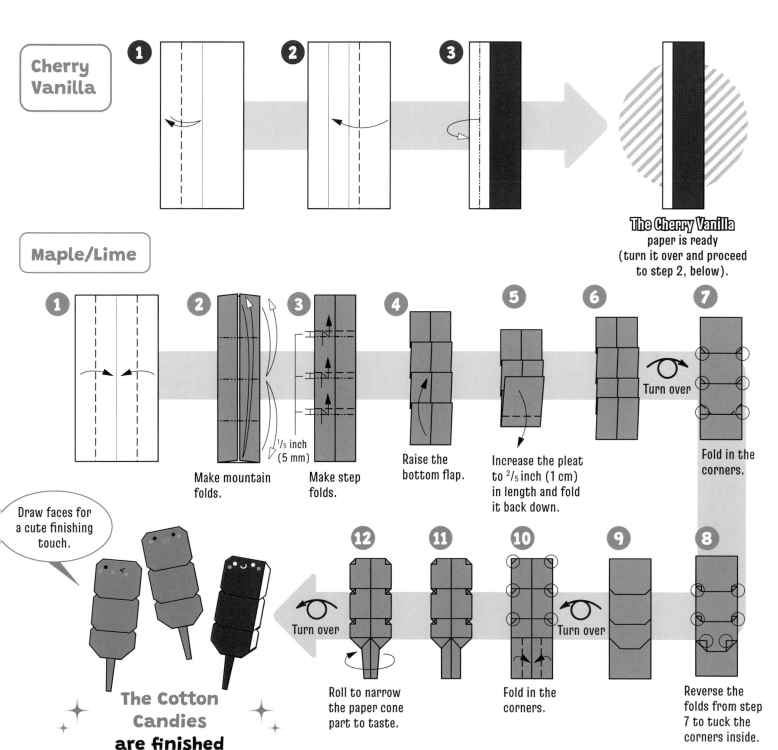

Lollipops

Photos on page 12

★ Origami Papers:
One per Lollipop

Your favorite color

★ Tools

Scissors   Felt-tip pen

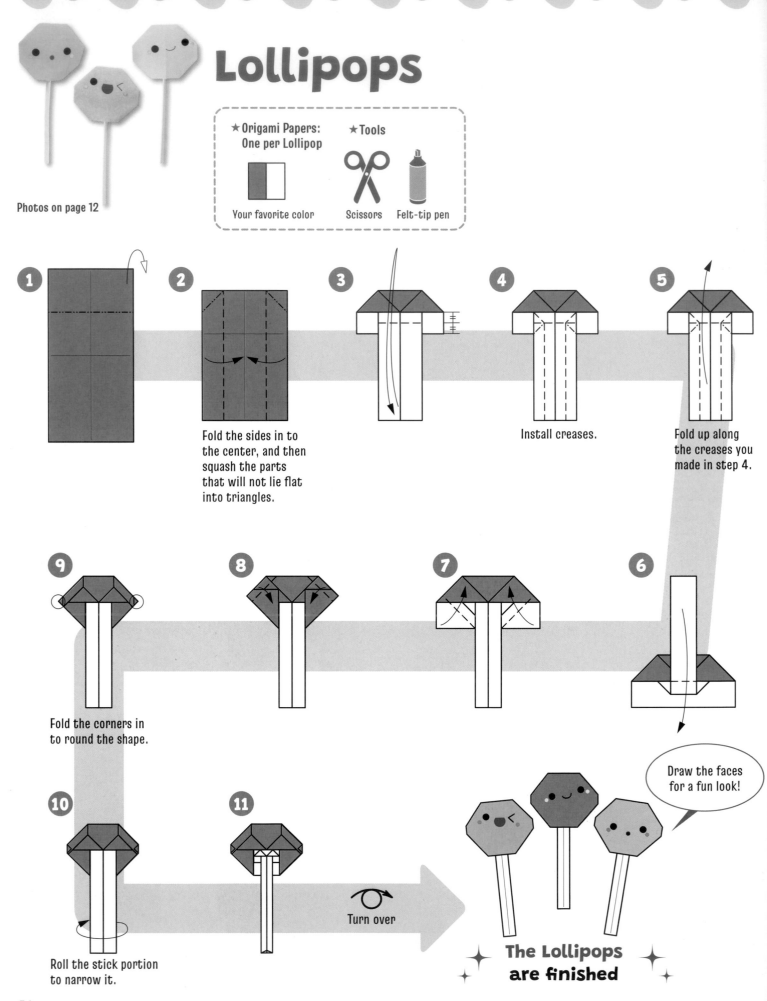

1

2 Fold the sides in to the center, and then squash the parts that will not lie flat into triangles.

3

4 Install creases.

5 Fold up along the creases you made in step 4.

6

7

8

9 Fold the corners in to round the shape.

10 Roll the stick portion to narrow it.

11

Turn over

Draw the faces for a fun look!

The Lollipops are finished

Photo on page 13

Cupcake

★ Origami Papers:
One per Cupcake

★ Tools

Your favorite color

Scissors

Felt-tip pen

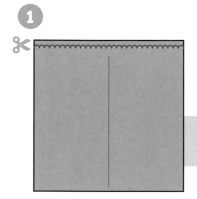

1 Cut the upper side with scissors in a scalloped line. If you don't have scalloping shears, you can cut a larger scalloped line freehand with ordinary scissors.

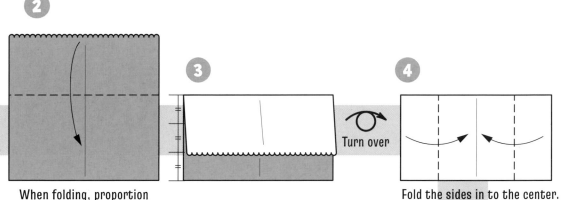

2 When folding, proportion the shaded side to the white side in a 2:1 ratio (see step 3).

3 Turn over

4 Fold the sides in to the center.

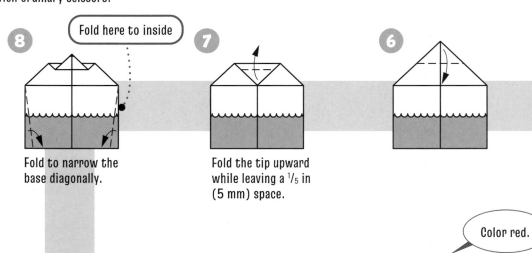

8 Fold here to inside

Fold to narrow the base diagonally.

7 Fold the tip upward while leaving a 1/5 in (5 mm) space.

6

5

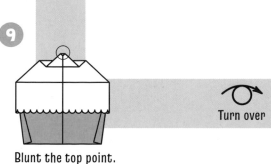

9 Blunt the top point.

Turn over

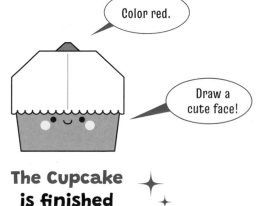

Color red.

Draw a cute face!

The Cupcake is finished

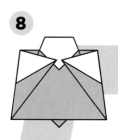

Photo on page 13

Pudding

★Origami Papers:
One per Pudding

Your favorite color

★Tools

Scissors

Felt-tip pen

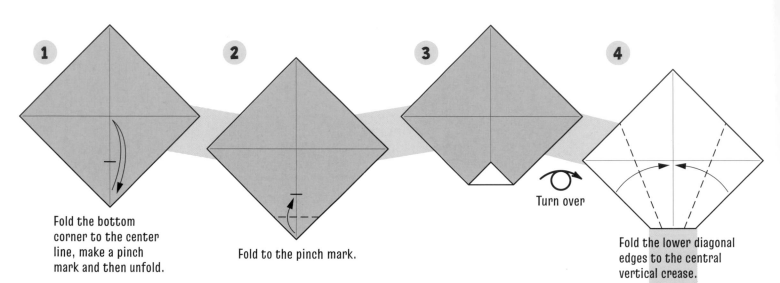

1
Fold the bottom corner to the center line, make a pinch mark and then unfold.

2
Fold to the pinch mark.

3
Turn over

4
Fold the lower diagonal edges to the central vertical crease.

8
Turn over

7
Fold the circled parts to almost meet in the center.

6
Fold upward to pair the circled locations.

5
Color in the topping. Draw lines on the whipped cream and add a cute face!

9
Draw a line that defines the edge of the topping.

10
Swing the whipped-cream flap to the front. Open the sides and trim away the part of the top flap that falls below the edge of the topping drawn in step 9.

11

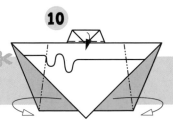

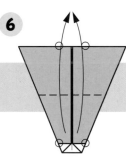

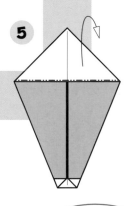

✦ **The Pudding** ✦
✦ **is finished** ✦

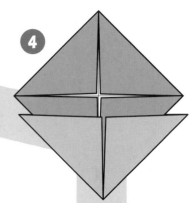

Donut

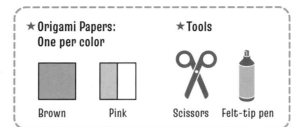

★Origami Papers:
One per color

Brown   Pink

★Tools

Scissors   Felt-tip pen

Photo on page 13

1

Prepare a Blintz Base
(refer to page 22).
Set aside.

2

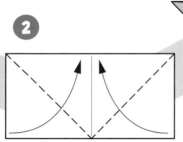

Fold the lower corners of the
secondary-color half sheet
diagonally to meet in the middle
of the top edge.

3

4

Nest the full-sheet part from
step 1 into the half-sheet
part from the previous step.

5

Mountain fold the
central corners inside.

6

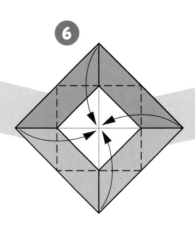

7

Open back up.

8

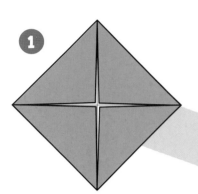

Install pinch marks.

9

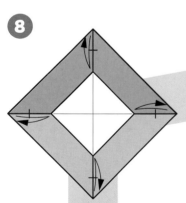

Fold the tips to the pinch marks, and
then fold the flaps in to the center.

10

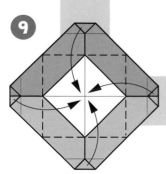

³/₅ inch (1.5 cm)

³/₅ inch (1.5 cm)

Fold the corners behind
to round the shape.

Draw a cheerful
face!

Adhere the triangular
tabs from step 10 to the
back with glue or tape
to make the front bulge
realistically.

**The Donut
is finished**

Rice Balls and Plate

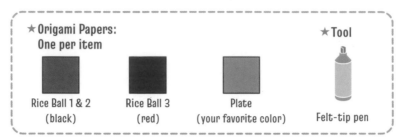

★ Origami Papers:
One per item

★ Tool

Rice Ball 1 & 2
(black)

Rice Ball 3
(red)

Plate
(your favorite color)

Felt-tip pen

Photo on page 14

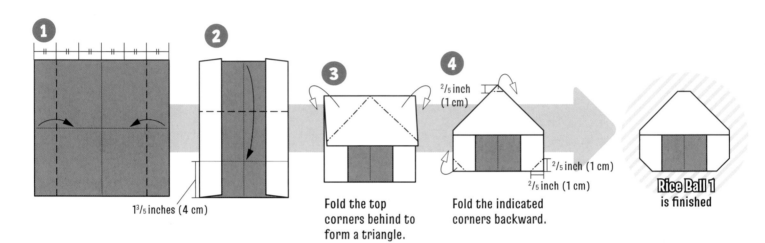

3 Fold the top
corners behind to
form a triangle.

4 Fold the indicated
corners backward.

²/₅ inch (1 cm)

²/₅ inch (1 cm)
²/₅ inch (1 cm)

1³/₅ inches (4 cm)

Rice Ball 1
is finished

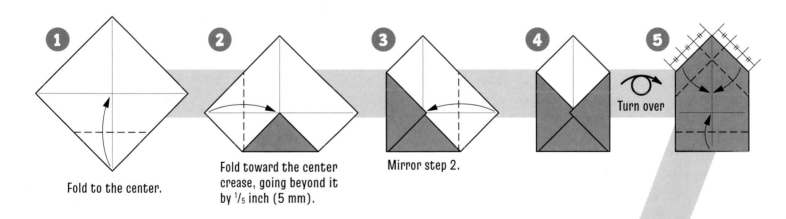

1 Fold to the center.

2 Fold toward the center
crease, going beyond it
by ¹/₅ inch (5 mm).

3 Mirror step 2.

4

5 Turn over

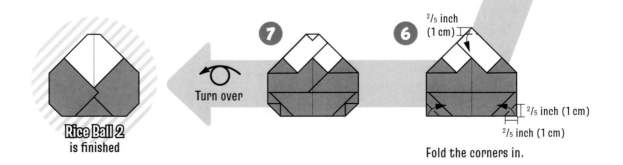

Rice Ball 2
is finished

7 Turn over

6 Fold the corners in.

²/₅ inch
(1 cm)

²/₅ inch (1 cm)

²/₅ inch (1 cm)

Refer to the Blintz Base (page 22).

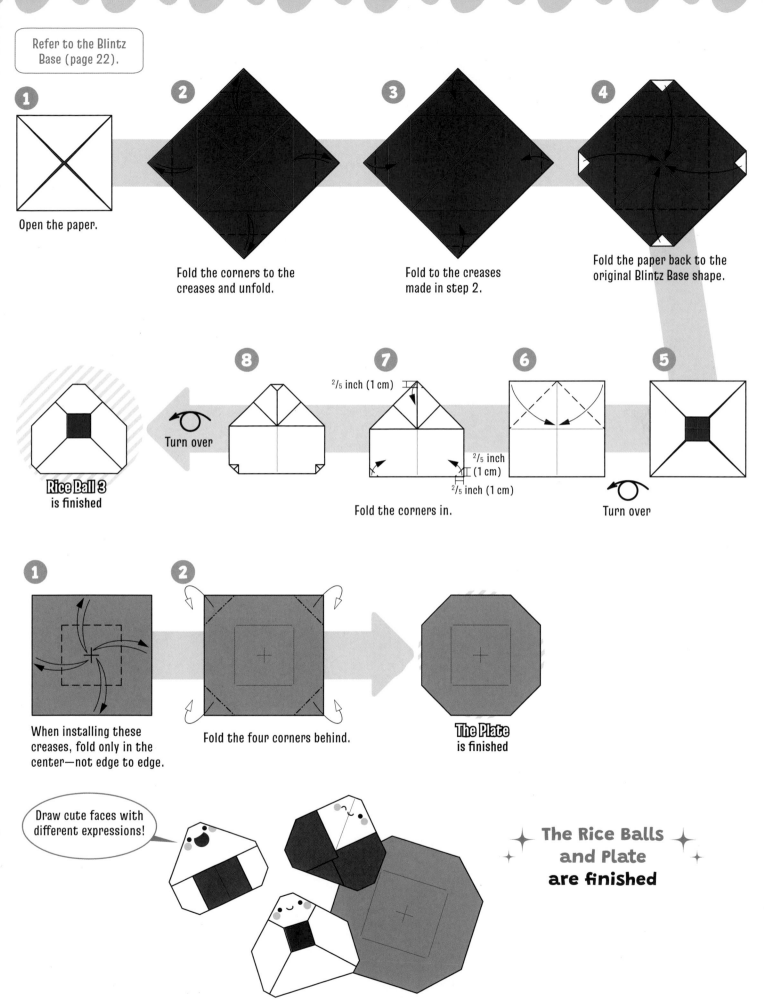

1 Open the paper.

2 Fold the corners to the creases and unfold.

3 Fold to the creases made in step 2.

4 Fold the paper back to the original Blintz Base shape.

5

Turn over

6

7 Fold the corners in.

²/₅ inch (1 cm)

²/₅ inch (1 cm)

²/₅ inch (1 cm)

8

Turn over

Rice Ball 3 is finished

1 When installing these creases, fold only in the center—not edge to edge.

2 Fold the four corners behind.

The Plate is finished

Draw cute faces with different expressions!

✦ **The Rice Balls** ✦ **and Plate** **are finished**

Fried Shrimp

Photo on page 15

★ **Origami Papers:** One per Shrimp

★ **Tool**

Gold

Felt-tip pen

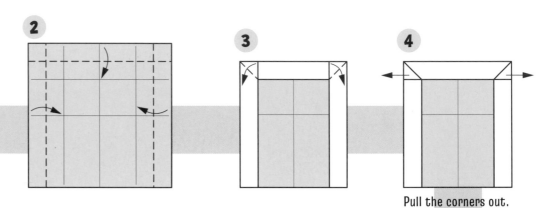

1 Install creases.

2

3

4 Pull the corners out.

8

7 ⅖ inch (1 cm) Grasp the corners to pull them out.

6 Turn over

5

Draw the face and color in the tail.

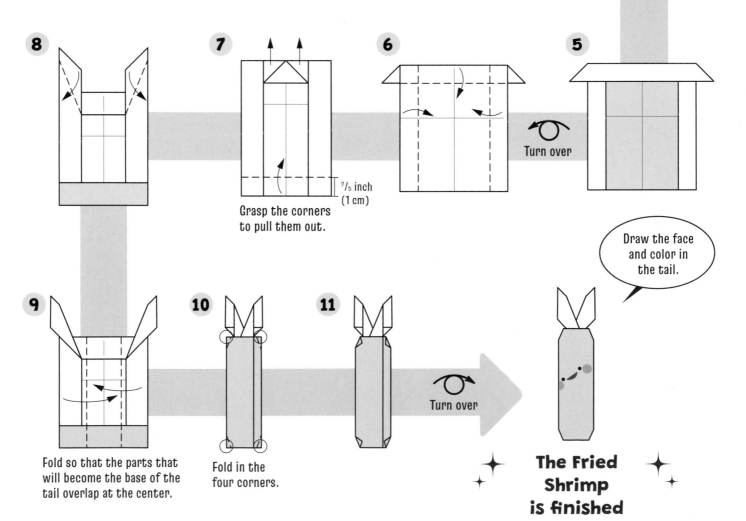

9 Fold so that the parts that will become the base of the tail overlap at the center.

10 Fold in the four corners.

11

Turn over

The Fried Shrimp is finished

60

Sunny-side up Egg

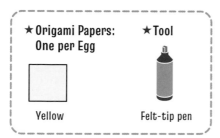

Photo on page 15

★Origami Papers:
One per Egg

Yellow

★Tool

Felt-tip pen

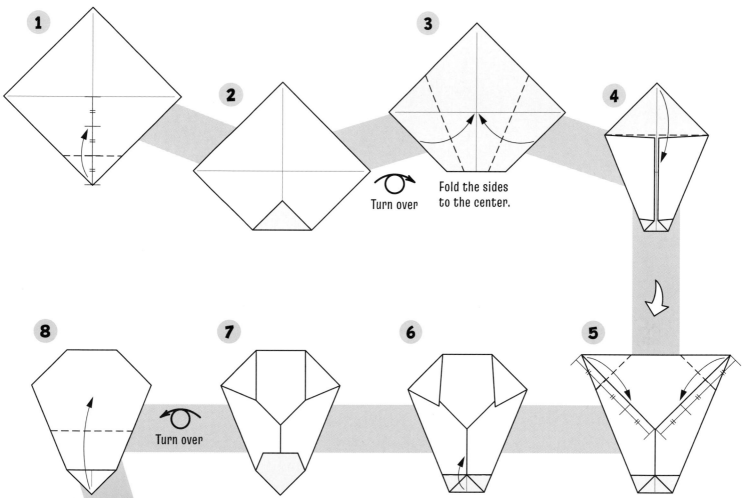

1

2

Turn over

3

Fold the sides
to the center.

4

5

6

Fold the yellow portion upward, causing the
triangular flap to swing forward from behind.

7

Turn over

8

Fold to bring the egg-
yolk part to the middle.

9

Fold the circled corners
behind to round the shape.

Draw the cheery
face with pens!

It's more
realistic if the
yolk's position is
not exactly
centered!

★ **The Sunny-side**
up Egg
is finished ★

Smoked Salmon

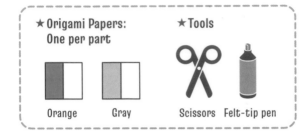

Photo on page 15

★ Origami Papers:
One per part

Orange   Gray

★ Tools

Scissors   Felt-tip pen

1 Overlap the orange and gray half sheets together (with the colors facing outward) before you begin. Fold the top edges to the middle.

2 Fold in half.

3 ³/₄ inch (2 cm) Fold diagonally.

4 Turn over

5

6 Fold diagonally to bring the corners together.

7 ³/₄ inch (2 cm) Bring the points indicated by the circles together. Squash the portion that will not lie flat.

8

9 Turn over

Draw the face with pens!

The Smoked Salmon is finished

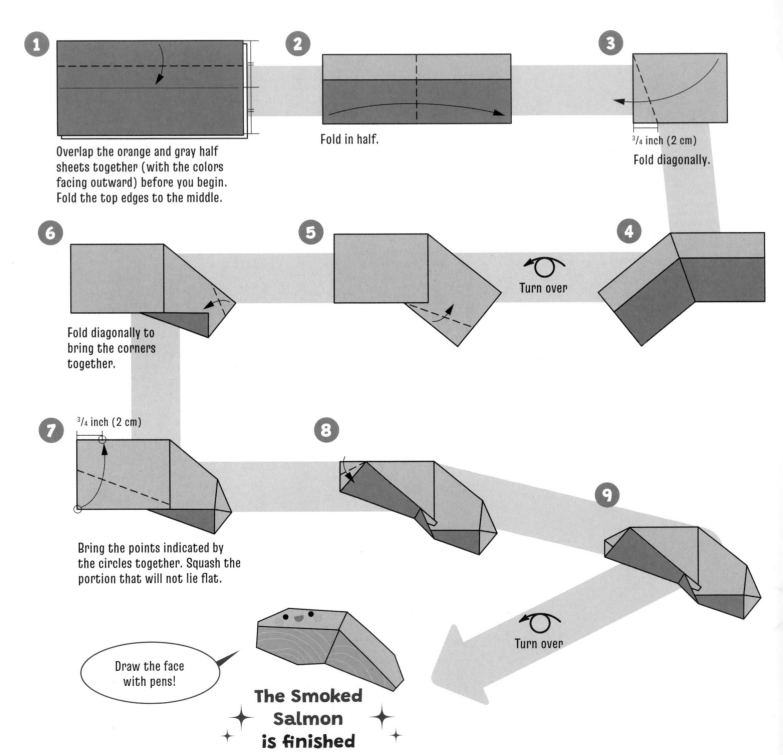

Omelet Rice

Photo on page 15

★ Origami Papers:
One per part

Rice (yellow)

Ketchup (red)

★ Tools

Scissors   Felt-tip pen

Rice

1 3/5 inch (1.5 cm)
3/5 inch (1.5 cm)

Fold the top and bottom corners to 3/5 inch (1.5 cm) away from the center.

2 Fold the paper in half.

3 3/4 inch (2 cm) 3/4 inch (2 cm)

Fold to intersect the corners marked with circles.

4 Tuck the protruding flaps inside.

5 Fold in the tips of the corners.

6 Turn over

The Rice is finished

Ketchup

1 Fold the paper into thirds.

2

3

4

The Ketchup is finished

How to assemble

The Ketchup part should straddle the Rice part.

Draw the face with pens!

The Omelet Rice is finished

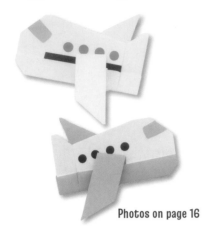

Airplane

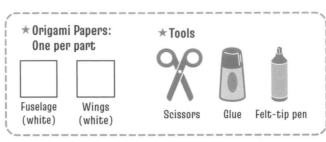

★Origami Papers:
One per part

Fuselage
(white)

Wings
(white)

★Tools

Scissors   Glue   Felt-tip pen

Photos on page 16

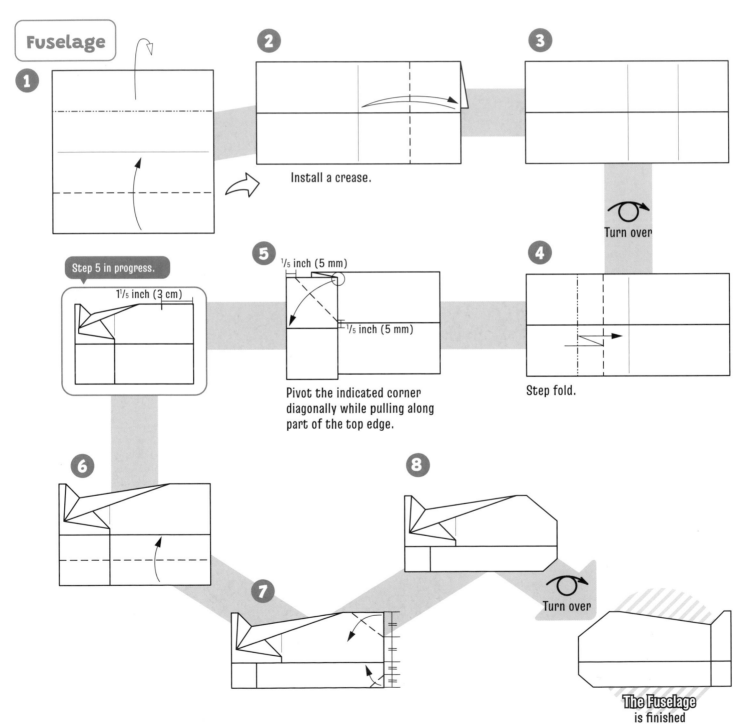

Fuselage

1

2

Install a crease.

3

Turn over

4

Step fold.

Step 5 in progress.

1 1/5 inch (3 cm)

5

1/5 inch (5 mm)

1/5 inch (5 mm)

Pivot the indicated corner
diagonally while pulling along
part of the top edge.

6

7

8

Turn over

The Fuselage
is finished

Wings

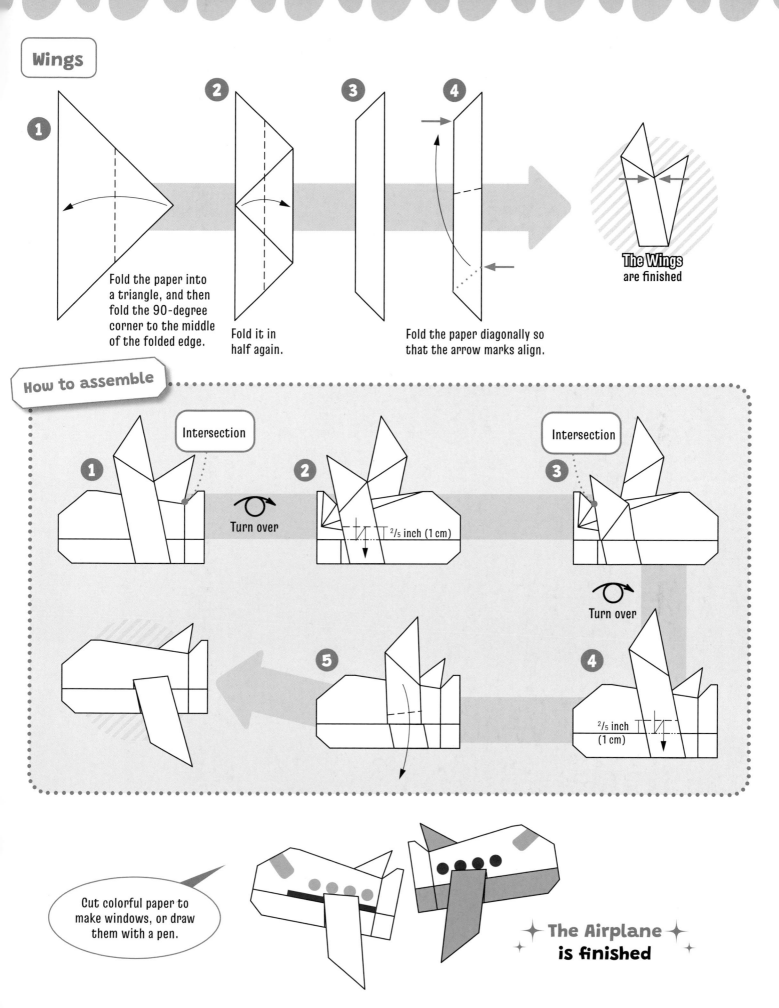

1 Fold the paper into a triangle, and then fold the 90-degree corner to the middle of the folded edge.

2 Fold it in half again.

3

4 Fold the paper diagonally so that the arrow marks align.

The Wings are finished

How to assemble

1 Intersection

Turn over

2 ²/₅ inch (1 cm)

3 Intersection

Turn over

4 ²/₅ inch (1 cm)

5

Cut colorful paper to make windows, or draw them with a pen.

✦ **The Airplane** ✦ **is finished**

Bullet Trains

Photos on page 16

★Origami Papers:
One per Train

★Tool

Blue   Light yellow   Felt-tip pen

Stop here if making a passenger car.

Bullet Train A

1

2

Fold behind so that the upper strip of white paper that results is the same width as the lower blue strip. Look ahead to step 3.

3

Turn over

7

1/5 inch (5 mm)

Fold the flap to the right so that it extends past the current right vertical edge by 1/5 inch (5 mm).

6

Fold a triangle, and then fold in a small portion of the tip.

5

Open, forming a triangle.

4

8

Fold the top flap diagonally.

9

Fold a triangle while pulling the inner part.

10

Turn over

Bullet Train A
is finished

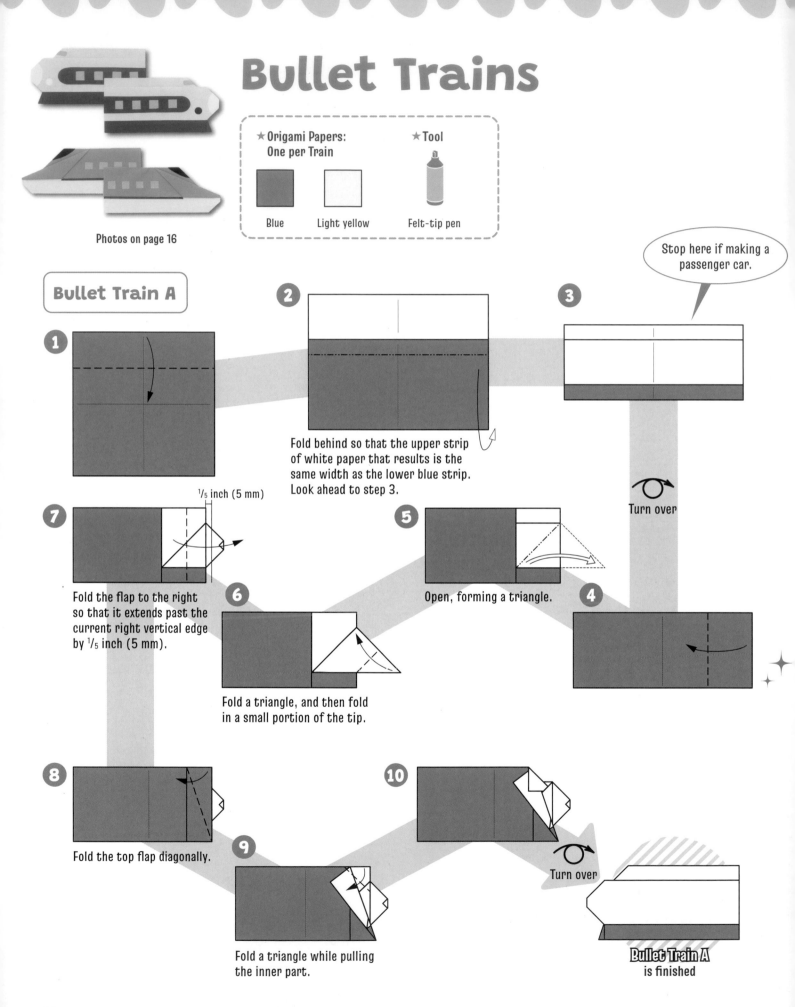

66

Bullet Train B

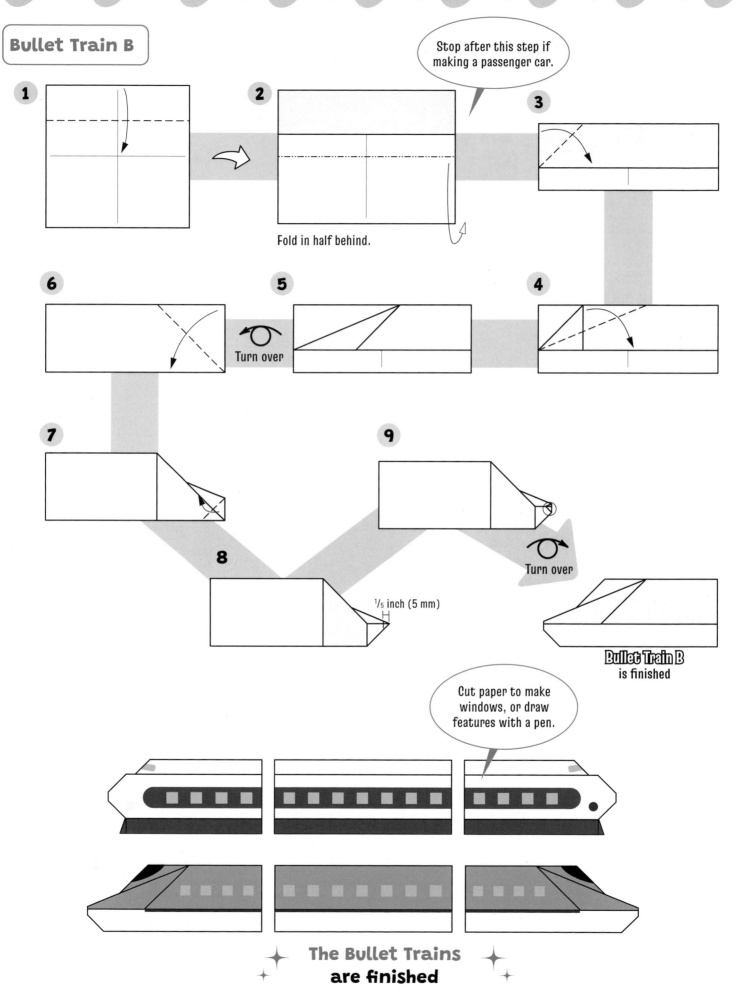

1

2

Fold in half behind.

3

Stop after this step if making a passenger car.

4

5

Turn over

6

7

8

1/5 inch (5 mm)

9

Turn over

Bullet Train B is finished

Cut paper to make windows, or draw features with a pen.

★ **The Bullet Trains** ★
are finished

67

Police Car and Ambulance

Photos on page 16

★ Origami Papers:
One per part

| Police Car Base (black) | Police Car Roof (white) | Ambulance Base (white) | Ambulance Roof (white) |

★ Tools

Scissors Glue Felt-tip pen

Police Car Base

Refer to Basic Form B (page 22).

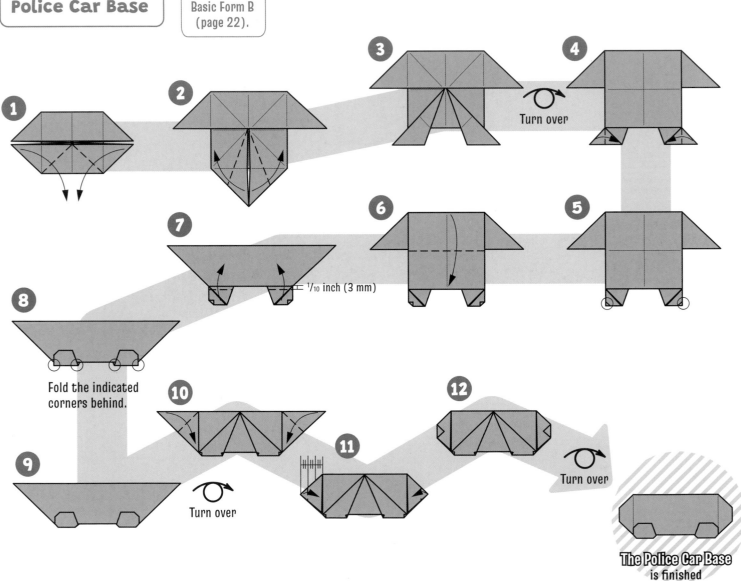

1

2

3

4 Turn over

5

6

7 — 1/10 inch (3 mm)

8 Fold the indicated corners behind.

9 Turn over

10

11

12 Turn over

The Police Car Base is finished

Police Car Roof

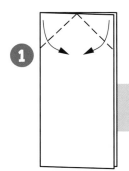

1 Fold the paper in half vertically. Fold the top edge into a point.

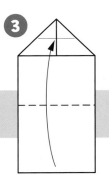

2 Make a crease.

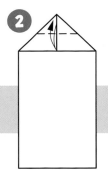

3 Fold the bottom edge up to match the crease from step 2.

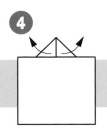

4 Spread open the triangle formed in step 1.

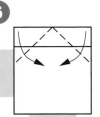

5 Refold the triangle, this time incorporating the top layout.

6

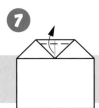

7 Fold up, leaving a gap.

8 Fold down a small portion of the tip.

9

Turn over

The Police Car Roof is finished

Ambulance Base

Refer to the Police Car Base through step 10.

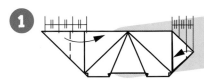

1

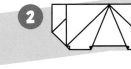

2

Flip over

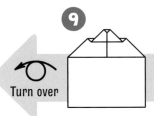

The Ambulance Base is finished

Color the tires black.

Ambulance Roof

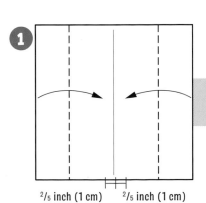

1 Fold the edges to fall $^2/_5$ inch (1 cm) short of the central crease.

$^2/_5$ inch (1 cm) $^2/_5$ inch (1 cm)

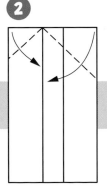

2

3 Fold the lower flap up to a position where the top peak extends about $^3/_5$ inch (1.5 cm) beyond the edge.

$^3/_5$ inch (1.5 cm)

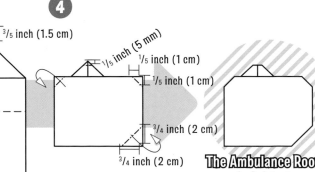

4 Fold the corners behind.

$^1/_5$ inch (5 mm)
$^1/_5$ inch (1 cm)
$^1/_5$ inch (1 cm)
$^3/_4$ inch (2 cm)
$^3/_4$ inch (2 cm)

The Ambulance Roof is finished

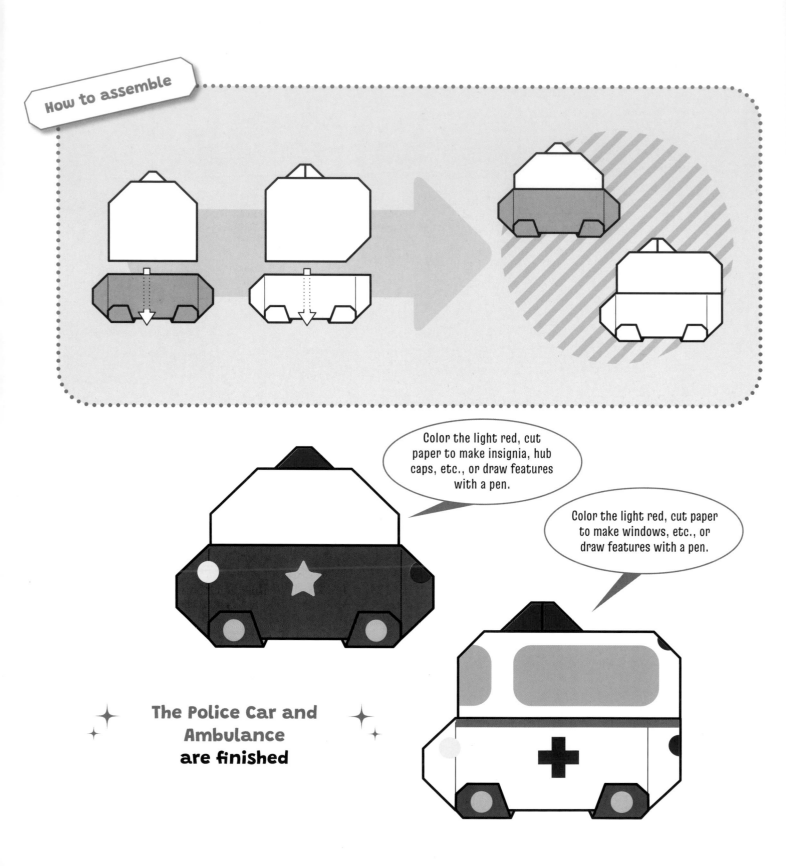

Color the light red, cut paper to make insignia, hub caps, etc., or draw features with a pen.

Color the light red, cut paper to make windows, etc., or draw features with a pen.

✦ **The Police Car and Ambulance are finished** ✦

Fire Truck

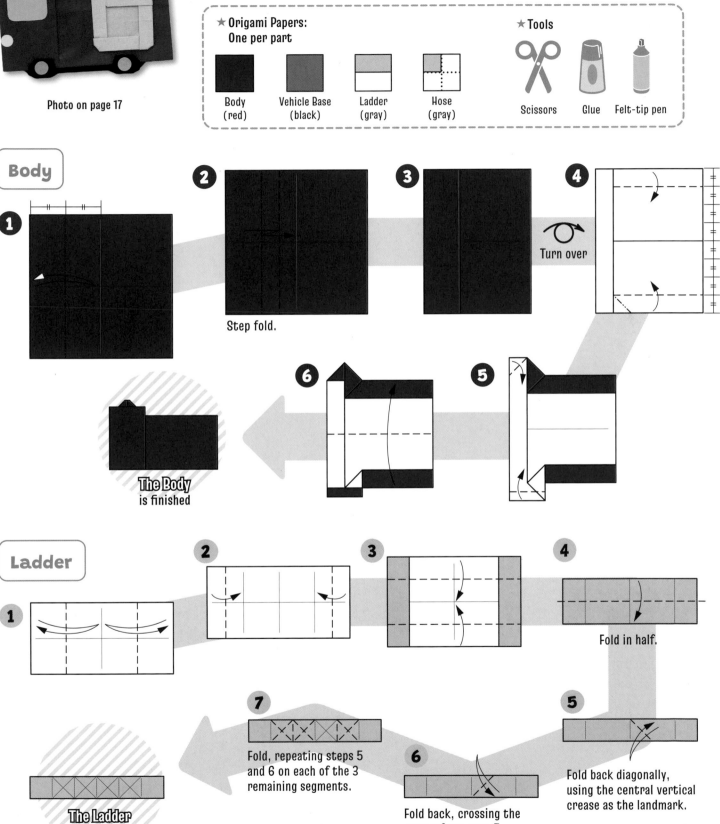

Photo on page 17

★ Origami Papers:
One per part

Body (red)   Vehicle Base (black)   Ladder (gray)   Hose (gray)

★ Tools

Scissors   Glue   Felt-tip pen

Body

1

2 Step fold.

3

4 Turn over

5

6

The Body is finished

Ladder

1

2

3

4 Fold in half.

5 Fold back diagonally, using the central vertical crease as the landmark.

6 Fold back, crossing the crease from step 5.

7 Fold, repeating steps 5 and 6 on each of the 3 remaining segments.

The Ladder is finished

Hose

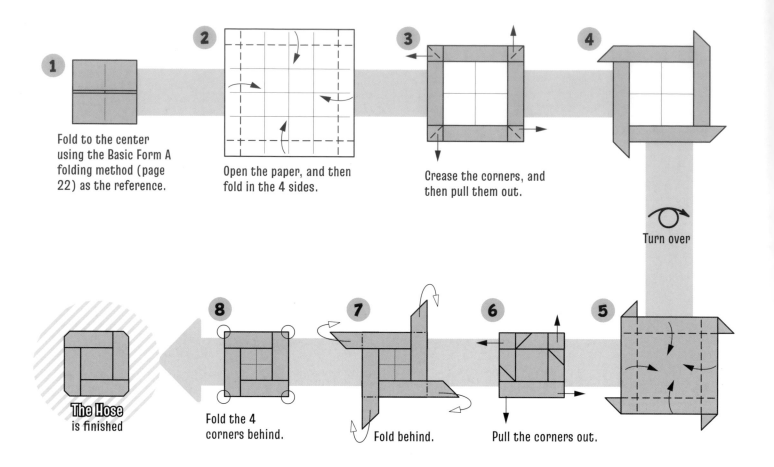

1 Fold to the center using the Basic Form A folding method (page 22) as the reference.

2 Open the paper, and then fold in the 4 sides.

3 Crease the corners, and then pull them out.

4

Turn over

5

6 Pull the corners out.

7 Fold behind.

8 Fold the 4 corners behind.

The Hose is finished

How to assemble

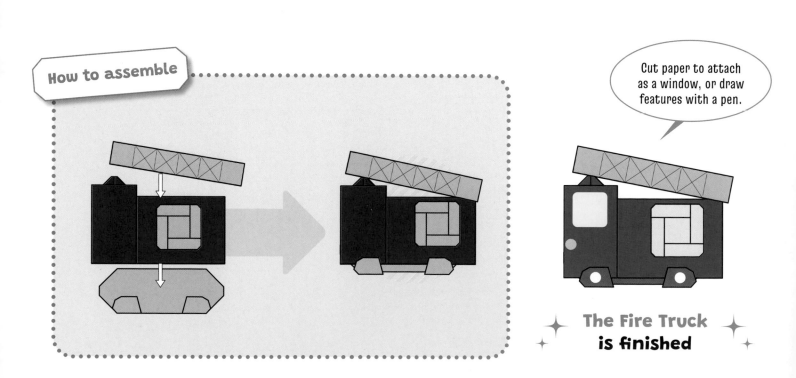

Cut paper to attach as a window, or draw features with a pen.

The Fire Truck is finished

Backhoe

★ Origami Papers:
One per part

Body (yellow)	Track (gray)	Arm and Bucket (yellow)

★ Tools

Scissors   Glue   Felt-tip pen

Photo on page 17

Body Refer to Basic Form B (page 22).

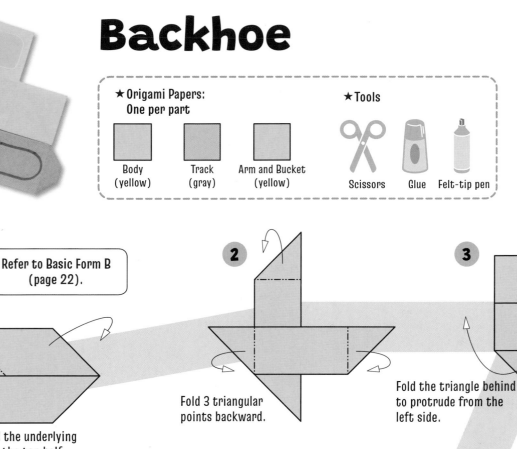

1 Mountain fold the underlying layer to pivot the top half into a vertical configuration.

2 Fold 3 triangular points backward.

3 Fold the triangle behind to protrude from the left side.

4

The Body is finished

Track Refer to Basic Form B (page 22).

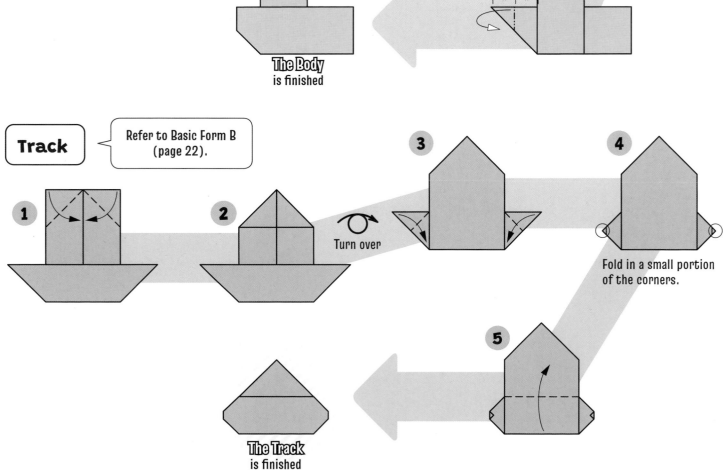

1

2

Turn over

3

4 Fold in a small portion of the corners.

5

The Track is finished

Arm and Bucket

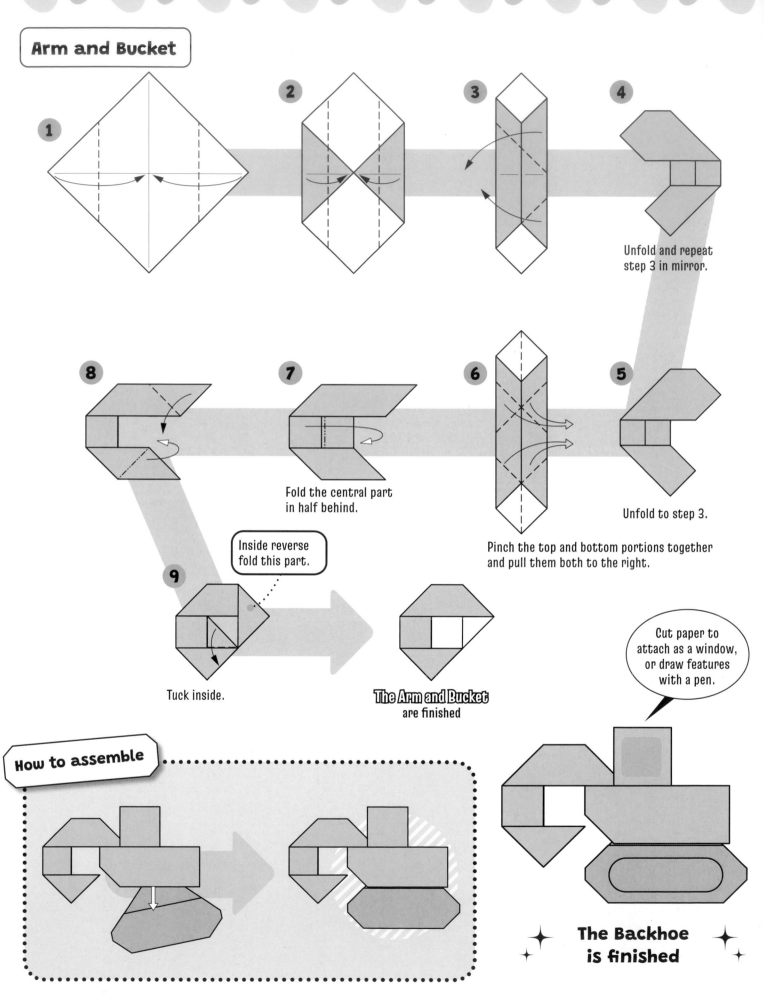

1

2

3

4

Unfold and repeat step 3 in mirror.

5

Unfold to step 3.

6

Pinch the top and bottom portions together and pull them both to the right.

7

Fold the central part in half behind.

8

9

Inside reverse fold this part.

Tuck inside.

The Arm and Bucket are finished

Cut paper to attach as a window, or draw features with a pen.

How to assemble

The Backhoe is finished

Photos on page 18

Flowers

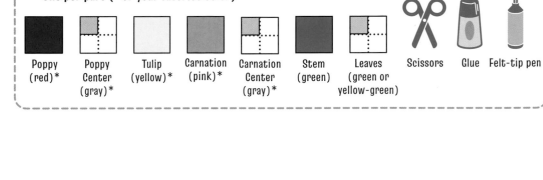

★ Origami Papers:
One per part (*or your favorite color)

| Poppy (red)* | Poppy Center (gray)* | Tulip (yellow)* | Carnation (pink)* | Carnation Center (gray)* | Stem (green) | Leaves (green or yellow-green) |

★ Tools

Scissors Glue Felt-tip pen

Poppy

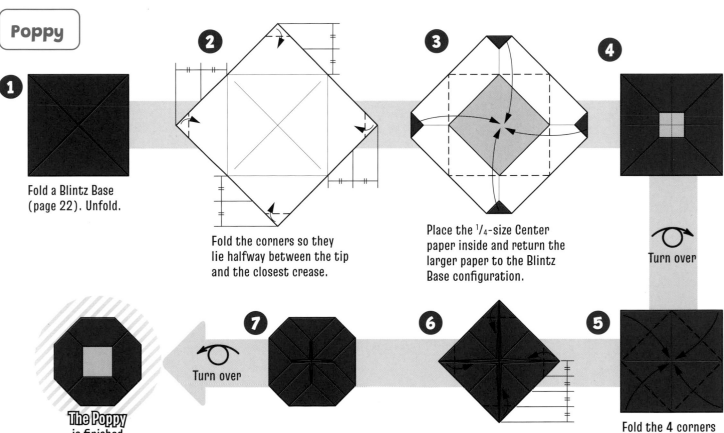

1 Fold a Blintz Base (page 22). Unfold.

2 Fold the corners so they lie halfway between the tip and the closest crease.

3 Place the 1/4-size Center paper inside and return the larger paper to the Blintz Base configuration.

4 Turn over

5 Fold the 4 corners to the center.

6

7 Turn over

The Poppy is finished

Carnation

Begin by folding up to step 4 of the Poppy instructions above.

1 Fold the 4 corners to the center.

2

3 Fold behind.

Rotate

The Carnation is finished

Tulip

Refer to Basic Form B (page 22)

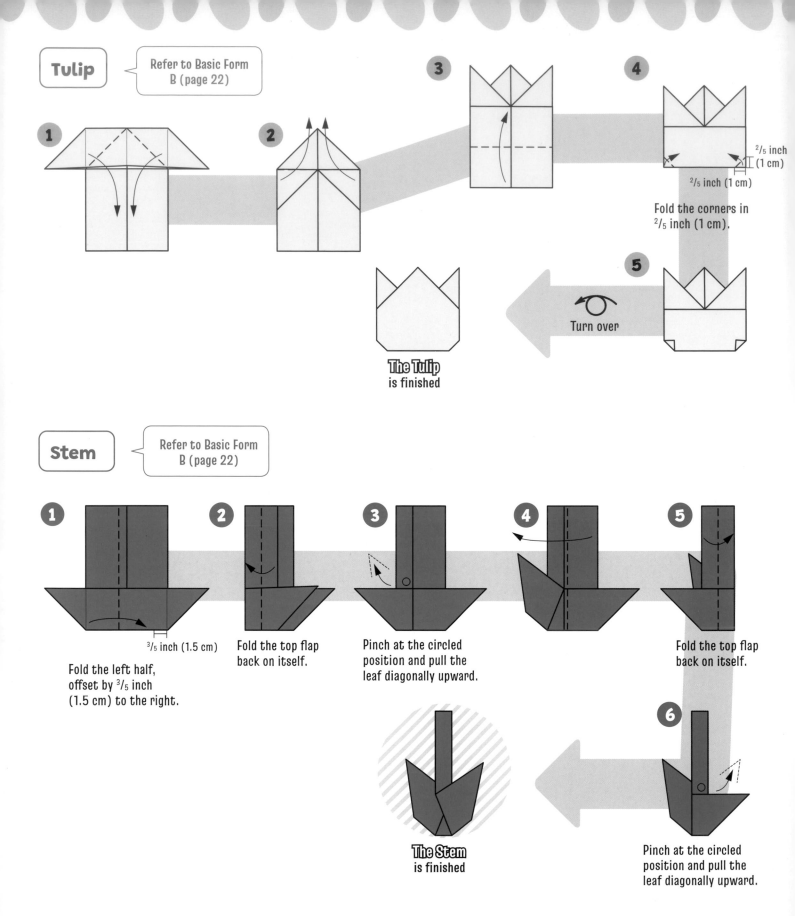

1

2

3

4

²/₅ inch (1 cm)

²/₅ inch (1 cm)

Fold the corners in ²/₅ inch (1 cm).

5

Turn over

The Tulip is finished

Stem

Refer to Basic Form B (page 22)

1

³/₅ inch (1.5 cm)

Fold the left half, offset by ³/₅ inch (1.5 cm) to the right.

2

Fold the top flap back on itself.

3

Pinch at the circled position and pull the leaf diagonally upward.

4

5

Fold the top flap back on itself.

6

Pinch at the circled position and pull the leaf diagonally upward.

The Stem is finished

Leaves

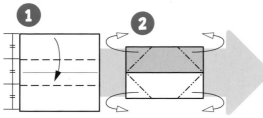

Fold the two pieces of
green and yellow-green
on top of each other.

The Leaves
are finished

How to assemble

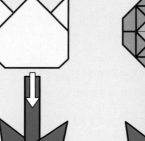

Fold the leaves with one-quarter size
paper and combine with the stems,
folded from a separate sheet.

Glue each flower onto a stem.

If you reduce the size of
the flower paper to one
quarter of a sheet, it will
become a small flower!

Draw faces with
a pen!

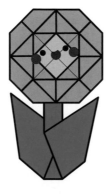

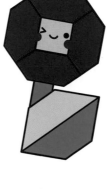

**The Flowers
are finished**

I hope you've enjoyed learning how to fold lots of cute origami models with fun drawn-on faces. The photos and detailed instructions mean that even beginners can easily make the models. Share what you've learned with your friends!

This book contains carefully selected and re-edited versions of popular models from Naoko Ishibashi's *Easy Origami Playtime for Children* and *Children's Origami Playtime*, previously published in Japanese.

About the author

Naoko Ishibashi lives in Kashiwa City, Chiba Prefecture, Japan. She became involved with character origami through her childcare studies, work and parenting experiences. She is fascinated by the idea of expressing cuteness through origami. She opened her own origami school and has fulfilled commissions for origami artwork. Her repertoire continues to grow, and she is the author of several books on the subject of origami in Japanese.

Published by Tuttle Publishing, an imprint of Periplus Editions (HK) Ltd.

www.tuttlepublishing.com

ISBN 978-4-8053-1676-4

Lady Boutique Series No. 4699
ISHIBASHI NAOKO KATAN! KODOMO NO ORIGAMI ASOBI
Copyright © 2018, Boutique-sha, Inc.
English translation rights arranged with Boutique-sha, Inc.
through Japan UNI Agency, Inc., Tokyo

Staff (Original Japanese edition)
Author Naoko Ishibashi
Editing Maruyama Ryohei
Photographer Harada Mari, Kitamura Yusuke
Book Design Yoshie Fujishiro (JV Communications)
Editor Shimura Satoru
Issuer Naito Akira

English translation © 2021 Periplus Editions (HK) Ltd
Translated from Japanese by HL Language Services

Printed in China   2209EP
26 25 24 23 22   10 9 8 7 6 5 4 3 2

Distributed by
North America, Latin America & Europe
Tuttle Publishing
364 Innovation Drive
North Clarendon
VT 05759-9436 U.S.A.
Tel: (802) 773-8930
Fax: (802) 773-6993
info@tuttlepublishing.com
www.tuttlepublishing.com

Japan
Tuttle Publishing
Yaekari Building 3rd Floor
5-4-12 Osaki Shinagawa-ku
Tokyo 141 0032
Tel: (81) 3 5437-0171
Fax: (81) 3 5437-0755
sales@tuttle.co.jp
www.tuttle.co.jp

Asia Pacific
Berkeley Books Pte. Ltd.
3 Kallang Sector, #04-01
Singapore 349278
Tel: (65) 6741-2178
Fax: (65) 6741-2179
inquiries@periplus.com.sg
www.tuttlepublishing.com

TUTTLE PUBLISHING® is a registered trademark of Tuttle Publishing, a division of Periplus Editions (HK) Ltd.

"Books to Span the East and West"

Tuttle Publishing was founded in 1832 in the small New England town of Rutland, Vermont [USA]. Our core values remain as strong today as they were then—to publish best-in-class books which bring people together one page at a time. In 1948, we established a publishing office in Japan—and Tuttle is now a leader in publishing English-language books about the arts, languages and cultures of Asia. The world has become a much smaller place today and Asia's economic and cultural influence has grown. Yet the need for meaningful dialogue and information about this diverse region has never been greater. Over the past seven decades, Tuttle has published thousands of books on subjects ranging from martial arts and paper crafts to language learning and literature—and our talented authors, illustrators, designers and photographers have won many prestigious awards. We welcome you to explore the wealth of information available on Asia at **www.tuttlepublishing.com**.